JAMES MADISON
1751 - 1836

Chronology—Documents—Bibliographical Aids

Edited by
IAN ELLIOT

Series Editor
HOWARD F. BREMER

1969
OCEANA PUBLICATIONS, INC.
Dobbs Ferry, New York

© Copyright by Oceana Publications, Inc. 1969
Library of Congress Catalog Card Number 76-90902
SBN 379-12068-2

Printed in the United States of America

CONTENTS

BIBLIOGRAPHICAL AIDS

EDITOR'S FOREWORD

Every attempt has been made to cite the most accurate dates in this Chronology. Diaries, documents, letters, and similar evidence have been used to determine the exact date. If, however, later scholarship has found such dates to be obviously erroneous, the more plausible date has been used. Should this Chronology be in conflict with other authorities, the student is urged to go back to original sources as well as to such careful biographers as Arthur Stanley Link.

This is a research tool compiled primarily for the student. While it does make some judgments on the significance of the events, it is hoped that they are reasoned judgments based on a long acquaintance with American History.

Obviously, the very selection of events by any writer is itself a judgment.

The essence of these little books is in their making available some pertinent facts and key documents *plus* a critical bibliography which should direct the student to investigate for himself additional and/or contradictory material. The works cited may not always be available in small libraries, but neither are they usually the old, out of print, type of book often included in similar accounts.

CHRONOLOGY

1751

March 16   Born, Port Conway, Virginia. Father: James Madison; mother, Nelly Rose Conway Madison.

1762

June 14   First payment of tuition at Donald Robertson School in King and Queen County, Virginia. This would date the start of Madison's formal schooling to shortly after his 11th birthday. He remained there for more than five years. Before entering the Robertson school, he studied at home.

1767

September 9   Final payment of tuition at Donald Robertson School. About this date, Madison left the school and spent one or two years studying with the Rev. Thomas Martin, who came to live with the Madisons in Montpelier. A graduate of Princeton, Martin was instrumental in persuading Madison to enroll there.

1768

May 20   Dolley Payne (Dolley Madison) born to John and Mary Coles Payne, in Guilford County, North Carolina. Her name is often incorrectly spelled as "Dolly."

1769

August   Attended the College of New Jersey (now known as Princeton). The exact date of Madison's entrance is not known. The fact that he was a leader of the American Whig Society there, which was founded in June, 1769, has led many scholars to assume that he entered in May at the beginning of the term. Probably, he entered later.

1771

September 25   Graduated from Princeton with a Bachelor of Arts degree.

October   Remained in Princeton for several months after graduation, until ill health health forced his return home.

1772

Spring   Returned to Montpelier, where he spent the next few years convalescing.

1773

November   Prepared for the Bar. Although he procured law books at this time, it is not known that he ever practiced law or was admitted to the Bar.

1774

May-July   Escorted his younger brother to Princeton. During this trip, Madison journeyed to rural New York. It was his first contact with an agricultural society virtually free of slavery.

December 2   Entered public life by being appointed one of 15 members of the Orange County Committee of Safety, a revolutionary committee created by the Continental Congress. James Madison Sr. was also named and served as chairman. Although barred from military service because of his health, the younger Madison was active in raising men and supplies for the country.

1775

May 3   Joined Orange County military company for the purpose of marching on Williamsburg to capture the gunpowder seized by the British Governor, Lord Dunmore. The Orange County company did not succeed, however, for the simple reason that Patrick Henry had beaten them to it.

1776

May 6   Delegate to Williamsburg convention, which declared for independence and set up a state government.

May 15   Convention declared the United Colonies to be free and independent states.

July 4   Congress in Philadelphia issued Declaration of Independence, a document which owes much in impetus, if nothing else, to Virginia's declaration.

October   Served in the House of Delegates of the Virginia Legislature. His two most important contributions were the help he gave in writing religious freedom into the statute law and his general support of Jefferson's progressive program.

November 30   Appointed by House of Delegates to a committee of six whose purpose was to examine enrolled bills and to make sure that the promulgated laws agreed with the passed bills.

1777

April

Defeated for re-election to the House of Delegates. The most widely accepted reason for his defeat was that he refused to give the voters free whiskey.

November 13

Elected by his fellow legislators to the "Privy Council or Council of State," which guided the Governor's actions and with him managed the state's part in the war; took office January 14, 1778.

1778

Spring

Elected to the House of Delegates by the freeholders of Orange County, the same voters who one year earlier had defeated him because of his refusal to buy votes with whiskey.

1779

December 14

Elected to the Continental Congress by the Virginia Legislature.

1780

March 18

Arrived in Philadelphia for the Continental Congress, which convened March 20.

March 23

Elected a member of the Board of Admiralty. It was a time consuming task and Madison resigned on June 6.

October 6

Elected chairman of a committee to write instructions to John Jay, in Madrid, in defense of the Western territories and the right to navigate the Mississippi. The final draft was passed with little or no opposition on October 17.

October 23

Appointed to a standing committee set up to correspond with the commanding officer in the South and report defense measures for that region. This was an important committee at the time, since there was a step-up in operations in the South, caused by General Gates' defeat in South Carolina.

1781

March 5

Argued unsuccessfully against the "chaos clause" of the

Articles of Confederation, which required the affirmative votes of either seven or nine states to carry any legislative question. Madison preferred a rule permitting decisions to be made by a majority of states once a quorum had been reached. This rule was finally adopted on May 29, 1787, at the Constitutional Convention, at which Madison was present.

May 2   Congress debated Madison's committee report on Congressional procedural matters. In essence, the debate concerned Federal power versus states' rights. Madison came out strongly for federal government and federal coercion of states.

June 6   Wrote legislation submitted to Congress which instructed the American peace negotiator to acede to no peace treaty which did not secure the independence of all thirteen states. Although the motion passed, it was reversed two days later by a resolution which left boundaries to the discretion of the peace negotiator.

1782

September 19   Attacked Congress' plan to send Henry Laurens, former president of Congress, to Paris as part of the peace delegation. Madison argued that Laurens was unfit to be an American Minister because he had written a document compromising the United States while being held captive by the British.

September 20   Defeated on Laurens issue.

1783

April   Became engaged to 16-year-old Kitty Floyd, daughter of a New York delegate. The engagement, however, was broken in August. The exact circumstances are not known, but presumably Madison did not initiate the action.

April 18   Congress adopted Madison revenue plan, which called for an impost to be raised by the states for the Federal government.

June 12   Congress adopted a resolution by Madison that "the true interest of these state requires that they should be as little as possible entangled in the politics and controversies of European nations." This was a forerunner of Washington's famous warning in the Farewell Address.

September 3   Peace treaty with Great Britain signed in Paris, word of which reached Washington at the end of October.

October   During this month, Madison pushed in Congress for a decision to make Georgetown the national capital. The final decision, a decade later, was the fulfilment of Madison's original plan.

October 25   Spent last day in Congress. His fourth yearly term came to an end on November 2 and in December he left for Montpelier.

1784

May 12   Took seat in Virginia House of Delegates and was made chairman of the committee on commerce and a member of the committees on religion, privileges and elections, propositions and grievances, and justice.

August   Received a gift from his father of 560 acres in Montpelier.

Left Virginia for a tour of the Northeastern states.

September 15   Left New York for a tour of the New York State Indian country, with Marquis de Lafayette, whom he had met by chance in Baltimore.

October   Returned for session of Virginia Legislature. During the session, his main preoccupation was to fight a move to establish Christianity as a state religion. He was finally able to guide an old 1779 bill of Jefferson's, which was concerned with religious liberty, to victory.

1786

February 16   James Monroe, who had recently toured New York's Mohawk Valley, suggested to Madison that they buy property there. They agreed to buy 900 acres at a dollar and a half an acre. Ten years later, Madison sold his share for a modest profit.

September   Attended Annapolis Convention.

November 1   Delivered speech in House of Delegates against paper money. Without taxes to back it, Madison said, paper money was unconstitutional and antifederal, infringing upon the right of Congress to regulate the value of coin.

The House declared against paper money by a lopsided vote.

November 7 Named by Assembly to a five-man delegation to the Confederation Congress in New York City. He attended the Congress from February to April, 1787.

1787

May 2 Left for Constitutional Convention in Philadelphia.

May 25 Convention began, with Washington unanimously elected chairman.

September 17 Convention ended. Madison played a leading role in casting the Constitution, so much so that he has been called the "Father of the Constitution." His most important contribution, perhaps, was the concept of national supremacy and local autonomy in a federal republic, ruled by people, with checks and balances to guard against legislative or executive tyranny and against impetuous legislation.

October 25 Reelected to the Continental Congress.

October 27 First number of **The Federalist** appeared in the New York **Independent Journal.** The purpose of this series of articles was to explain the Constitution and defend it against attack. Three men—Madison, Alexander Hamilton and John Jay—were the authors, although all articles were signed "Publius."

1788

June 2 Member of the Virginia Convention to ratify the Federal Constitution.

June 6 Spoke out against Patrick Henry who opposed ratification of the Constitution. Henry objected to the supremacy of the Federal government over Virginia, and threatened to pull southern Virginia out of the Union by secession.

June 25 Constitution ratified by Virginia. Madison was credited with guiding the Constitution to victory.

July 14 Presented Virginia's ratification to Congress in New York.

August 4 Voted for Baltimore as capital of the United States. His purpose was to prevent New York from being designated the permanent capital. The motion carried, but was shelved two days later.

August 11   Sent an honorary LLD by the president of Princeton.

October 31   Reelected to Congress with the help of his political enemy Patrick Henry, whose main desire was to keep Madison out of Virginia and out of the Senate.

November 13   The Virginia Legislature, under pressure from Henry, voted to readjust Madison's district to prevent his election. The new district contained the most rabid anti-Federalist localities. Henry obtained James Monroe to run against Madison.

1789

January   Spent two weeks with Monroe, traveling from county to county and debating the Constitution.

February 2   Defeated Monroe for seat in Congress.

March 4   Entered U. S. House of Representatives as Congressman from Virginia; until March 3, 1797.

April 8   Proposed duties on imports as a means of paying the national debt; later introduced an amendment limiting the duration of the import bill, to avoid the stigma of levying a perpetual tax. The proposal was passed overwhelmingly.

April 30   George Washington inaugurated first President of the United States; John Adams, Vice President.

May 5   Engineered a Congressional move advising against any styles or titles for the President and Vice President, other than those specified in the Constitution. This was in response to Adams' contention that the President should be called "His Highness the President of the United States and Protector of Their Liberties." Adams' proposal was quietly dropped.

May 19   Proposed that there be a Department of Foreign Affairs, a Treasury Department and a War Department, each to be headed by a Secretary appointed by the

President, by and with the advice and consent of the Senate, and removable by the President.

June 8   Introduced the subject of Constitutional amendments. After several months' debate, Congress adopted the Bill of Rights. The major part of this document was introduced by Madison.

1790

February 22   Defeated by Congress in his attempt to have the Federal government pay off both the original holders of government securities (for the most part, veterans and widows) and those who had bought the securities later at a deflated price. Madison found himself pitted against Hamilton in the first of many political battles.

December 13   Hamilton submitted plan for national bank. Successfully opposed by Madison in the House on the issue of constitutionality.

1791

May 23   Set out with Jefferson for tour of New York and Vermont; trip ended on June 15 in New York City.

1792

May 25   Asked by Washington in a letter to draft a farewell statement to the people. At the time, Washington was considering retirement after one term. Madison produced a preliminary draft of the famous Farewell Address, delivered by Washington on September 19, 1796.

August   French Republic conferred honorary citizenship on Madison, Washington and Hamilton. Only Madison accepted the honor.

December 5   Washington unanimously elected President for a second term.

1793

April 22   Washington signed "Proclamation of Neutrality" between Great Britain and France. Hamilton favored the measure, while Madison and Jefferson were strongly opposed to it.

August 24   First of a series of eight articles by Madison, written under the pseudonym "Helvidius," for the **Gazette of the United States.** The articles were written in response to an earlier series written by Hamilton, under the pseudonym "Pacificus" in favor of Washington's neutrality act.

1794

September 15   Married Dolley Payne Todd, in Jefferson County, Va. At the time of marriage, she was the widow of John Todd, by whom she had two sons, one of whom died in infancy. Her living son was named John Payne Todd.

November 9   Jay Treaty signed with Great Britain. Although the treaty covered many points of amity, commerce and navigation, it failed to require the British to renounce search or impressment.

December 26   Dolley Madison expelled by her Quaker congregation for marrying outside of her faith.

1796

April   Throughout April, Madison led the Republican forces in the House in a fight against Jay's treaty. He won one victory when the House upheld the right to reject the treaty if it so wished, but lost when the House narrowly voted to accept the treaty.

December 7   Presidential election held. Although some results were still in doubt, Adams appeared to be elected.

1797

February 8   Official counting of votes revealed the election of Adams as President and Jefferson as Vice President.

March 4   John Adams inaugurated President; Thomas Jefferson Vice President.

1798

June 25   Alien Act gave the President authority to expel aliens dangerous to the public safety or suspected of treasonable tendencies. The Act expired in 1802.

July 14   Sedition Act passed, providing fines and imprisonment for persons conspiring against the government and its laws, for attempting or aiding "insurrections, riots or unlawful assembly," and for "false, scandalous and malicious writing or utterances against the government." Although Adams was not active in its enforcement, the bill was undoubtedly aimed at suppressing political opposition. It resulted in the indictment of about 15 persons, 10 of whom were convicted.

December 24　Virginia Assembly adopted Madison's **Virginia Resolutions,** which were an attack on what Madison considered infractions of the Constitution by the Alien and Sedition Acts. These resolutions were written in conjunction with Jefferson's Kentucky Resolutions, which covered the same ground but were more emotional in tone and exhibited a more extreme assertion of state power.

1799

Spring　Elected to Virginia Legislature. During his term, Madison wrote a report on the Virginia Resolutions.

December 14　Washington died at Mount Vernon.

1800

January　Delivered report which defended the Virginia Resolutions clause by clause. The report was a bitter indictment of the Alien and Sedition Acts.

November　Elected a Presidential elector from Virginia by a vote of "340 odd to 7."

1801

February 17　Jefferson elected President over Aaron Burr, when deadlock in the House was finally broken after six days.

February 27　Madison's father, James Madison Sr., died.

March 4　Thomas Jefferson inaugurated President.

March 5　Nominated by Jefferson for post of Secretary of State.

May 2　Appointed Secretary of State; served until March 3, 1809.

July-October　Remained on his farm in Monticello. These summer retreats were taken by Madison every year for the next 16 years. Like Jefferson, Madison wished to be away from Washington during the season of malaria and bilious fevers. While Jefferson was in office, government affairs went smoothly during the summer since the two men were only 30 miles apart in Virginia.

1803

January 3　Complained to French Minister Louis Pichon that France was ignoring the United States in regard to its inquiries about American rights and interests on the Mississippi. Pichon received the impression—although it is doubtful that Madison was explicit about this—that the United States might be forced to ally itself with Great Britain to forestall Napoleon.

January 12   James Monroe appointed Minister to France to aid R. R. Livingston acquire the right of free navigation of the Mississippi.

January 14   Warned France through Pichon that France was not to provoke a forcible expansion of the United States beyond the Mississippi. Warnings such as this, and the one given on January 3, are thought to have had a decided influence on Napoleon.

April 18   Monroe appointed Minister to England for the purpose of securing a shipping treaty.

May 2   The Louisiana Purchase signed by Monroe and Livingston in France. Under the terms of the agreement, France transferred a vast area of western lands in return for 60 million francs and payment by the United States of debts incurred by France to American citizens. The total cost to the United States was 15 million dollars.

1804

February 24   Bill signed by Jefferson which added to the Mississippi customs district "all the navigable waters, rivers, creeks, bays and inlets lying within the United States, which empty into the Gulf of Mexico east of the Mississippi." This part of the bill was known as Section 4. Far more controversial was Section 11 which gave the President discretionary power to create a separate customs district embracing "the shores, waters and inlets of the bay and river of the Mobile" and other waterways east of the Mobile and westward to the Pascagoula. This section—it will be noted—did not contain the words "lying within the United States."

March 5   The Marquis de Casa Yrujo, Spanish Minister to the United States, protested strongly to Madison about Section 11. Yrujo vigorously defended Spain's title to West Florida.

March 19 In an effort to ease the crisis, Madison wrote to Yrujo that Section 11 was subordinate to Section 4 and thereby was limited by implication to places "lying within the United States."

May 18 Napoleon became emperor of France.

May 30 Jefferson erected a Mobile revenue district with Fort Stoddard (a few miles north of the Spanish-American border) as port of entry. In defining the district's limits, he inserted and italicized the phrase "lying wihin the boundaries of the United States." Despite this easing act, however, a bitter quarrel now existed between Yrujo and Madison.

June 23 Summoned British Minister Anthony Merry to inform him that officers of the British warships **Cambrian** and **Driver** had violated American neutrality by impressing 14 seamen from the **Pitt,** a British merchant ship in New York harbor. Madison demanded the return of the 14, an apology, and the delivery of the lieutenant who had insulted revenue and quarantine officers. Although the United States received a grudging apology, the ships remained outside New York harbor and continued to harrass shipping.

July 11 Hamilton mortally wounded by Aaron Burr in duel at Weehawken, N. J. Hamilton died the next day.

1805

May 23 Instructed Monroe, then in Spain, to ask Spain not to strengthen her military forces in the West Florida area (in return for which the United States would do likewise) and not to obstruct free access to the sea through the Mobile and other rivers. This produced no effect whatsoever.

July 23 Monroe arrived in London on the day of the Essex decision. This case changed earlier policy about "broken voyages" and the British began to seize American ships, often outside American harbors.

July 25 Left for Philadelphia with his wife for treatment of an ulcerated tumor on Dolley Madison's leg. During the next three months, Madison visited Washington only occasionally. It was the first time since Jefferson had become President that the two men were separated.

November 9   General Francisco Miranda arrived in New York to seek British and American help in liberating his native Venezuela from Spain. He subsequently had interviews with Madison and then made it seem as if the United States would covertly sanction an expedition against the Spanish in Venezuela.

December 23   Two armed ships left the United States for Port au Prince to obtain recruits for the liberation of Venezuela. A third armed vessel left on February 2.

1806

January   Published a 70,000 word pamphlet entitled **Examination of the British Doctrine, which subjects to capture a Neutral Trade Not Open in Time of Peace.** This pamphlet, published anonymously, was written in protest against the British practice of seizing American ships which were trading with French and Spanish colonies.

January 15   Yrujo, who had been asked to leave the United States "voluntarily" as a result of his bitter feud with Madison and his attempt to bribe a Federalist editor to print pro-Spanish news, was asked once again by Madison to leave Washington. Yrujo's response was to protest Madison's request to all foreign diplomats.

February   Received first intimations of Aaron Burr's plot to conquer Spanish territory west of the Mississippi and use it to form the nucleus of an independent republic.

February 6   Learned of Miranda's deception and one day later took steps to find out whether any persons now in the United States were liable to criminal prosecution. Two men were brought to trial but were acquitted. Some political damage was suffered by Jefferson and Madison.

April 18   Non-Intercourse Act provided that after November 15 certain articles of British growth or manufacture should not be imported from Great Britain or British colonies.

October   Informed that Burr was predicting and advocating separation of the West, that boats were being built for him and that General James Wilkinson, commander in chief of the U. S. Army and governor of upper Louisiana, was Burr's co-conspirator.

October 20 Wilkinson betrayed Burr by warning Jefferson of the plot.

December 31 Monroe concluded treaty with the British. Although the treaty provided for certain commercial and trade concessions, it failed to come up with any arrangement on impressment, the topic uppermost in the minds of American statesmen. This treaty was deemed so unsatisfactory by Madison and Jefferson that they refused to submit it to the Senate for ratification.

1807

February 1 Learned through dispatches that Monroe and Pinkney had agreed to leave out the matter of impressment from the British treaty.

March 3 Received copy of the British treaty.

June 22 American ship of war, **Chesapeake,** fired on by British cruiser, **Leopard,** 10 miles off Norfolk, Virginia, after refusing British demand to board for impressment. Three Americans were killed and four alleged deserters were removed after boarding.

July 6 Sent instructions to Monroe to demand a British disavowal of the Chesapeake affair and restoration of the four impressed seamen.

August 31 Burr found not guilty of treason at his trial in Richmond, Virginia. Presiding at the trial was Chief Justice John Marshall.

1808

January 21 Endorsed as a Presidential candidate by Virginia Legislature over Monroe.

January 23 Nominated for President by a Congressional caucus of Democratic-Republicans. Madison received 83 votes, compared to three votes each for Monroe and George Clinton of New York.

February 28   Met with Monroe, who defended his treaty with Great Britain as the best possible treaty under the circumstances.

December 7   At meeting of Electoral College, Madison received 122 votes and 12 states, while Federalist Charles Pinckney of South Carolina received 47 votes and 5 states.

1809

March 1   Non-Intercourse Act prohibited either British or French public ships from entering American waters unless in distress or on government business. However, the President was authorized to revoke the ban against either England or France should either of them cease to violate the neutral commerce of the United States.

TERM IN OFFICE

March 4   Inaugurated fourth President of the United States in the chamber of the House of Representatives. The path was administered by Chief Justice John Marshall. George Clinton of New York was inaugurated Vice President.

March 6   Robert Smith of Maryland appointed Secretary of State.

March 7   William Eustis of Massachussetts appointed Secretary of War; entered upon duties April 8.

April 19   Proclaimed that since the British Orders in Council were to be withdrawn on June 10, the United States would thereafter resume trade with Great Britain (the Erskine Agreement). This agreement, however, was rejected by the British when word finally reached England.

May 7   Paul Hamilton of South Carolina appointed Secretary of the Navy.

May 31   Dolley Madison held the first of her famous Wednesday night levees, with the President's house thrown open wide to invited friends and strangers.

June 26   John Quincy Adams, son of the second President, nominated to be Minister to Russia.

August 9   Signed a proclamation announcing that since the British

Orders in Council had not been withdrawn on June 10, the Non-Intercourse Act was restored.

September 30   General William H. Harrison negotiated treaty with the Indians at Fort Wayne by which he obtained nearly three million acres on the Wabash River above Terre Haut.

November 29   Presented first annual message to Congress.

1810

January 3   Asked for the revival of the expiring "Chesapeake crisis" law, which authorized him to require the states to arm and equip 100,000 militiamen.

May 1   Non-Intercourse Act repealed and replaced with Macon's Bill No. 2. This re-opened trade with England and France, but provided for non-intercourse against one should the other revoke its orders or decrees.

August 5   France announced the repeal of the Berlin and Milan decrees. Despite this action, however, France's actions continued at times to be highly provocative. As late as March, 1812, for example, American ships were being burned for trading with Portugal.

September 5   Sent order to authorities in West Florida directing the use of force to prevent and punish any incursion into West Florida by a convention army rumored to be on its way from Baton Rouge.

October 27   Signed a proclamation directing territorial officials to take possession of West Florida. The territory had been taken some two weeks earlier by General David Thomas, who seized the Spanish fort at Baton Rouge. The territory thereupon proclaimed itself to be "a free and independent state."

November 2   Proclaimed that France had met the requirements of the Macon Bill and that three months thereafter, unless Britain similarly revoked her Orders in Council, the Non-Intercourse Act of 1809 would be revived against her.

December 5   Delivered second annual message to Congress.

1811

January 3   Sent to the Capitol a secret message concerning all of

Florida. In it, Madison recommended a declaration which foreshadowed the Monroe Doctrine: "that the United States could not see without serious inquietude any part of a neighboring territory in which they have in different respects so deep and so just a concern pass from the hands of Spain into those of any foreign power."

January 15   Signed a bill and resolution, passed in secrecy, authorizing him to take possession of Florida from the Perdido River to the Atlantic Ocean, employing the Army, Navy and $100,000, provided an arrangement for delivering it was made with the local authority or in the event of attempted foreign occupation.

February 21   Vetoed a bill incorporating the Protestant Episcopal Church in the District of Columbia on the constitutional grounds that "Congress shall make no law respecting a religious establishment."

February 28   Vetoed a grant of land to the Salem, Mississippi Baptist Church because it represented a principle of supporting a religious institution with public funds.

March 2   Congress passed the Non-Importation Act (see November 2, 1810).

April 1   Robert Smith resigned as Secretary of State. He was asked to resign by Madison for the following reasons: incompetence, antagonism to Madison's policies, and a bitter feud with Secretary of the Treasury Gallatin. As a sop, Smith was offered the post of Minister of Russia. He accepted it at first and then later refused. His ouster left him feeling extremely bitter towards Madison.

April 2   Monroe appointed Secretary of State; entered upon duties April 6.

May 16   American frigate **President** severely damages British sloop-of-war **Little Belt** in battle off New York harbor.

July 22   French Minister officially informed by his government that France had released all American ships and their cargoes which had arrived in French ports after November 1.

November 5   Delivered third annual message to Congress.

November 7   General William Henry Harrison—later to become the 9th President—defeated Indian attackers under Tecumseh at Tippecanoe on the Wabash River. The event, with many American casualties, stirred up much American sentiment in the West to take Canada from the British.

November 12   Accepted a settlement of the "Chesapeake affair." The settlement was virtually a duplicate of the one negotiated by Erskine in 1809 and later repudiated by the British cabinet.

November 18   Appointed Joseph Story of Massachussetts and Gabriel Duvall of Maryland as Associate Justices of the Supreme Court.

December 11   William Pinkney of Maryland appointed Attorney General; entered upon duties January 6, 1812.

1812

January 11   With war close at hand, Madison signed a bill passed by Congress adding 25,000 troops to the regular complement of 4,000.

January 16   Informed Congress that Great Britain was known to be holding 6,200 impressed American seamen.

March 9   Submitted to Congress the "spy letters" of Captain John Henry, formerly of the British Army. The letters showed that while the United States was negotiating with Erskine in 1809, Henry had been sent by the British government to act as a secret agent in certain states—notably Massachussetts—to foment disaffection against the United States government, incite resistance to its laws and, finally, in concert with a British force, to destroy the Union and throw the Eastern region into a political connection with Great Britain.

March 31   Sent word to Congress that he would ask for a declaration of war if assured of Congressional support, but would not assume "the responsibility of declaring that we are prepared for war."

April 1   Asked Congress to order a general embargo on all ships now in port, or hereafter arriving, for a period of 60 days. Although Congress lengthened the embargo to 90 days, it nevertheless acted promptly and Madison signed the bill three days after requesting it. It was generally accepted that unless Great Britain drastically revised its policies on the high seas, the embargo was a prelude to war.

April 20 Vice President Clinton died in Washington, D. C. He was the first Vice President to die in office.

May 18 Democratic-Republican members of Congress voted unanimously to renominate Madison for President.

May 29 Democratic-Republicans of the New York State legislature unanimously nominated DeWitt Clinton, mayor of New York city, lieutenant governor and political boss, for the Presidency.

June 1 Sent Congress a message which reviewed the outstanding differences between the United States and Great Britain.

June 15 Senate rejected a motion to limit war against Great Britain to naval reprisals and privateering against British ships.

June 16 British Parliament suspended Orders in Council. This was, in effect, a complete capitulation to the United States. However, because of the poor communications of the time, war was nevertheless declared by the United States two days later.

June 17 Senate rejected a proposal to make war at sea against both Britain and France.

June 18 Signed a declaration of unrestricted war against Great Britain.

Commodores John Rodgers and Stephen Decatur and Captain Isaac Hull given "every belligerent right" on the high seas. Rodgers was directed to seek out and destroy two British warships, the **Belvidera** and the **Tartarus,** known to be cruising off Sandy Hook. Shortly thereafter, Rodgers (commanding the **President)** engaged in a running battle with the **Belvidera,** which finally escaped. These were the opening shots of the War of 1812.

July 9   In response to Congressional pressure, issued a proclamation which set aside a day in August for "public humiliation and prayer" for victory. Like Jefferson, who refused to issue thanksgiving proclamations, Madison regarded such proclamations as an encroachment of freedom of religion.

August   Throughout most of this month, Madison was visited in Washington by a number of Indian chiefs from the western territories. Among the tribes represented were the Sac, Fox, Sioux, Shawness and the three Osage tribes (Big, Little and Arkansas). Madison had two primary aims: to act as peacemaker between the tribes warring against each other, and to deter some tribes (notably the Sioux and Sacs) from joining the war on the side of the British.

August 12   Saw the full text of the repeal of the Orders in Council. Four days later, the British Minister argued for a suspension of hostilities; however, Madison and Monroe decided to wait until they saw what reaction Britain would have to the delcaration of war.

August 16   General William Hull surrendered Detroit and his entire army of 2,500, without firing a shot, to a smaller British force of 700 troops, including militia, and 600 Indians.

August 19   The American frigate **Constitution,** commanded by Captain Isaac Hull (the General's nephew), destroyed the British frigate **Guerriere.**

September 14   Replaced Brigadier General James Winchester with Major General William Henry Harrison as head of the Northwest Command.

September 15   Federalist leaders, meeting in New York, decided that no Federalist candidate could defeat Madison in the forthcoming election and that, instead, the Federalists would throw their support to DeWitt Clinton, the New York Republican.

November 4   Delivered fourth annual message to Congress.

November 5   Vetoed a naturalization bill because it was "liable to abuse by aliens having no real purpose of effectuating a naturalization."

December 3   Received 128 votes and 11 states to DeWitt Clinton's 89 votes and 7 states, for the Presidency.

December 11   Sent to Congress letters from Captain Decatur and Captain Jacob Jones reporting the victories of the frigate **United States** over the British frigate **Macedonia** and the sloop of war **Wasp** over the British sloop of war **Frolic.**

1813

January 1   Monroe appointed Secretary of War **ad interim.**

January 12   William Jones of Pennsylvania appointed Secretary of the Navy; entered upon duties January 19.

January 13   John Armstrong of New York appointed Secretary of War; entered upon duties February 5.

January 28   The Russian Minister, Andre de Daschkoff, offered unofficially the mediation of the Russian Emperor to solve differences between the United States and England. Since the offer was unauthorized, Madison made no reply. About one month later, an official offer was made and Madison accepted.

February 22   Sent to Congress a letter and documents from Captain William Bainbridge relating the victory of his frigate, the **Constitution,** over the British frigate **Java.**

February 24   Submitted to Congress a British proclamation providing for the supply of the West Indies and other colonies by licensed importations from "the ports of the Eastern States exclusively." Madison claimed that this was an attempt to dissolve the ties of allegiance within the United States.

March 4   Inaugurated for second term as President, with Elbridge Gerry of Massachusetts as his Vice-President.

April 28   York, capital of Upper Canada, surrendered to an American force. Many of the city's public buildings were burned.

May 9

Secretary of the Treasury Gallatin and Senator James Bayard of Delaware sailed for peace mission based on Russian mediation. During Gallatin's absence, Secretary of the Navy Jones performed the Treasury's duties.

May 25

Sent special message to Congress reviewing the conduct of the war and the prospects of Russian mediation.

September 13

Master Commandant (later Captain) Oliver Perry defeated a British fleet in the Battle of Lake Erie.

December 7

Delivered fifth annual message to Congress.

1814

January 6

Sent Congress his acceptance of Lord Castlereagh's offer of direct peace negotiations. Castlereagh had rejected Russian mediation in the summer of 1813 and had proposed direct negotiation in either London or Gothenburg, Sweden. Madison chose Gothenburg.

February 9

George Washington Campbell of Tennessee appointed Secretary of the Treasury.

February 10

Richard Rush of Pennsylvania appointed Attorney General; entered upon duties February 11.

March 17

Jonathan Meigs Jr. of Ohio appointed Postmaster General; entered upon duties April 11.

March 31

Recommended to Congress a relaxation of the strict embargo and non-importation laws.

June 17

Granted a full pardon to all persons who deserted the Army of the United States, provided such persons surrender themselves within three months.

June 29

Instructed all armed vessels of the United States not to interfere with neutral vessels bound for any port under the jurisdiction of the United States.

July 1

Summoned cabinet to consider the defense of Washington.

July 2

Brigadier General William Winder given command of the Washington-Baltimore command.

August 22

Learned, along with the rest of Washington, that British

troops were advancing overland on Washington. Madison left on horseback to encourage the troops defending the capital.

August 24   Visited American troops stationed at Bladensburg, Maryland, to forestall capture of Washington. Madison was the first and only President to face enemy gunfire while in office.

August 25   British burned all non-military public buildings in Washington except the combined General Post Office and Patent Office. Among the casualties were the President's mansion and the Library of Congress. The British later gave the burning of York (see April 28, 1813) as an excuse for the burning of Washington.

August 27   Returned to Washington, the British having left for their ships.

September 4   Secretary Armstrong, much criticized for his lack of defense of Washington, resigned.

September 11 American naval forces decisively defeated the British in the Battle of Lake Champlain.

September 12-13 Francis Scott Key composed "The Star Spangled Banner" while watching an unsuccessful British attack on Fort McHenry in Baltimore.

September 20 Delivered second annual message to Congress.

September 27 Appointed James Monroe Secretary of War; entered upon duties October 1.

October 6   Appointed Alexander James Dallas of Pennsylvania Secretary of the Treasury; entered upon duties October 14.

November 7   General Andrew Jackson entered Pensacola, took the town from the British, redelivered it to the Spanish and left for Mobile and New Orleans.

November 15   Signed two war bills—one appropriating $600,000 for twenty 16-gun warships, and the other authorizing him to borrow $3 million for current expenses.

November 23   Vice-President Elbridge Gerry of Massachussetts died in office. He was the second Vice-President to die in office, the other being Clinton who served during Madison's first term.

December 15 The Federalists—particularly those from New England— met in Hartford, Connecticut. One of their aims was to break the existing Union, thus allowing individual states to make treaties with foreign powers (such as, of course, a peace treaty with Britain). Although the delegates castigated Madison and made demands upon him in the form of Constitutional amendments, they backed away from outright secession.

December 19 Benjamin William Crowinshield of Massachussetts appointed Secretary of the Navy; entered upon duties January 16, 1815.

December 24 Treaty of Ghent was signed by Britain and the United States, bringing to an end the War of 1812. Although the provisions of the treaty included the return of captured territory, the appointment of commissions to settle the disputed northeastern boundary and steps toward the abolition of the slave trade, there was nothing done about impressment, right of search, blockade, neutral rights or indemnities, fisheries or navigation of the Mississippi.

1815

January 8 Andrew Jackson defeated British in the Battle of New Orleans, with 700 British killed (including their commander), 1,400 wounded and 500 captured. American losses: seven killed, six wounded.

February 6 Granted a full pardon to the pirates, led by Jean Laffite, who congregated near the mouth of the Mississippi, in recognition of their help in the Battle of New Orleans.

February 14 Received Treaty of Ghent from Monroe. It was ratified by the Senate one day later.

February 17 Proclaimed the end of the War of 1812.

February 18 In a special message to Congress, warned against a sudden and general revocation of war measures.

February 23   Requested—and obtained from Congress—a declaration of war against the Dey of Algiers who in 1812 "began open and direct warfare" against American citizens and still held some of them in captivity.

February 28   Reappointed Monroe Secretary of State.

June 30   Agreement reached on a peace treaty between the United States and the Dey of Algiers.

August 1   William Harris Crawford of Georgia appointed Secretary of War; entered upon duties August 8.

December 5   Delivered seventh annual message to Congress.

December 12   Ordered the removal of all persons who had unlawfully taken possession of or settled upon public lands.

1816

April 10   Signed the bill creating the Second Bank of the United States—24 years after he led the fight to deny the establishment of the First Bank on the grounds that it was unconstitutional.

October 22   W. H. Crawford appointed Secretary of the Treasury.

December 3   Delivered last annual message to Congress.

December 25   Made life member of American Colonization Society, which was formed to settle free Negroes in Africa. In 1833, Madison was elected president of the Society; he was too ill and too enfeebled to do more than serve in name only.

1817

March 3   Served last day in office as President. One of his final acts was to veto a bill for internal improvements because he though it unconstitutional.

LATER LIFE AND RETIREMENT

March 4   Monroe inaugurated President; Daniel Tompkins of New York, Vice President.

March 6   Presented with the resolutions of a mass meeting by the Mayor of Washington. The resolutions praised Madison for maintaining political and civil liberties while prosecuting the war.

April 6   Left Washington for Montpelier, Virginia.

1818

May   Delivered address as president of the Agricultural Society of Albermarle, to which he had been elected. In the address, Madison recommended many practices regarded as revolutionary, such as reforestation, contour plowing, soil depletion and use of fertilizer.

1819

February 26   Met with Jefferson at Montpelier as members of the Board of Visitors responsible for founding the University of Virginia. The two ex-Presidents were given the responsibility of securing a faculty.

1824

November 4   Met Lafayette at Jefferson's home in Monticello. Lafayette—the sole surviving general of the American Revolution—had returned to America for a final visit, 40 years after he had taken leave of Washington.

1826

July 4   Jefferson and John Adams both died. Shortly after Jeffersons' death, Madison succeeded him as rector of the University of Virginia.

1828

January   At Virginia's anti-Jackson convention, delegates unanimously nominated a Presidential ticket of Madison and Monroe. Both former Presidents refused the nomination when informed of it.

1829

February 11   Madison's mother, Nelly Conway Madison, died.

October 5   As delegate to the convention to revise Virginia's constitution—his last official public service—nominated Monroe for the convention's presidency. He and Chief Justice John Marshall escorted Monroe to the chair.

1830

October   The **North American Review** published a 3,500-word letter from Madison in which he repudiated the use of the

Virginia Resolutions (see December 24, 1798) to justify opposition to a protective tariff proposed by Congress. Since the Resolutions championed the right of a state to oppose what it considered unconstitutional acts by Congress, and since Madison was author of those Resolutions, his name was being increasingly invoked by those who wished to "nullify" the proposed tariff.

1831

July 4   James Monroe died in New York City, five years to the day after the deaths of Jefferson and Adams.

1832

November 24   South Carolina convention adopted nullifying ordinance forbidding federal officers to collect duties within the state, prohibiting appeals to the Supreme Court and decreeing that any forcible attempt to execute tariff laws would sever South Carolina's connection with the Union. The convention based nullification on Madison's Virginia Resolutions. A few days later, Madison wrote to friends in the Virginia legislature protesting the distortion of his ideas.

December 1   Virginia legislature took up the question of nullification. The pattern was repeated: Madison's name invoked by opponents of the tariff, while Madison's friends protested that his ideas were being distorted. The legislature finally reaffirmed the Resolutions but denied the course taken by South Carolina. Resistance to the tariff collapsed in South Carolina shortly thereafter.

1835

July 6   Chief Justice Marshall died. Madison was elected to succeed him as president of the Washington National Monument Association.

1836

June 28   Died at Montpelier; buried in family plot there.

1849

July 12   Dolley Madison died in Washington, D. C.; buried in Montpelier.

DOCUMENTS

THE FEDERALIST—NUMBER 10
November 23, 1787

Article Number 10 written by Madison, is probably the most famous of all The Federalist articles. In it, Madison presents a study of the origin of political parties and the sources of faction in government. One of the principal effects of this article has been to promote an economic interpretation of history. Some critics believe that, because of this article, Madison is the real author of the Marxian doctrine of economic determinism. The date above refers to the publication, not the writing, of the article.

THE SIZE AND VARIETY OF THE UNION AS A CHECK ON FACTION

To the People of the State of New York:

AMONG the numerous advantages promised by a well-constructed Union, none deserves to be more accurately developed than its tendency to break and control the violence of faction. The friend of popular governments never finds himself so much alarmed for their character and fate, as when he contemplates their propensity to this dangerous vice. He will not fail, therefore, to set a due value on any plan which, without violating the principles to which he is attached, provides a proper cure for it. The instability, injustice, and confusion introduced into the public councils, have, in truth, been the mortal diseases under which popular governments have everywhere perished; as they continue to be the favorite and fruitful topics from which the adversaries to liberty derive their most specious declamations. The valuable improvements made by the American constitutions on the popular models, both ancient and modern, cannot certainly be too much admired; but it would be an unwarrantable partiality, to contend that they have as effectually obviated the danger on this side, as was wished and expected. Complaints are everywhere heard from our most considerate and virtuous citizens, equally the friends of public and private faith,

and of public and personal liberty, that our governments are too un-
stable, that the public good is disregarded in the conflicts of rival
parties, and that measures are too often decided, not according to the
rules of justice and the rights of the minor party, but by the superior
force of an interested and overbearing majority. However anxiously
we may wish that these complaints had no foundation, the evidence
of known facts will not permit us to deny that they are in some degree
true. It will be found, indeed, on a candid review of our situation,
that some of the distresses under which we labor have been erroneously
charged on the operation of our governments; but it will be found, at
the same time, that other causes will not alone account for many of
our heaviest misfortunes; and, particularly, for that prevailing and increasing distrust of public engagements, and alarm for private rights,
which are echoed from one end of the continent to the other. These
must be chiefly, if not wholly, effects of the unsteadiness and injustice with which a factious spirit has tainted our public administrations.

By a faction, I understand a number of citizens, whether amounting
to a majority or minority of the whole, who are united and actuated
by some common impulse of passion, or of interest, adverse to the
rights of other citizens, or to the permanent and aggregate interests
of the community.

There are two methods of curing the mischiefs of faction: the one,
by removing its causes; the other, by controlling its effects.

There are again two methods of removing the causes of faction:
the one, by destroying the liberty which is essential to its existence;
the other, by giving to every citizen the same opinions, the same
passions, and the same interests.

It could never be more truly said than of the first remedy, that it
was worse than the disease. Liberty is to faction what air is to fire,
an aliment without which it instantly expires. But it could not be less
folly to abolish liberty, which is essential to political life, because it
nourishes faction, than it would be to wish the annihilation of air,
which is essential to animal life, because it imparts to fire its destructive agency.

The second expedient is as impracticable as the first would be unwise. As long as the reason of man continues fallible, and he is at
liberty to exercise it, different opinions will be formed. As long as
the connection subsists between his reason and his self-love, his opinions and his passions will have a reciprocal influence on each other:
and the former will be objects to which the latter will attach themselves. The diversity in the faculties of men, from which the right
of property originate, is not less an insuperable obstacle to a unifor-
mity of interests. The protection of these faculties is the first object
of government. From the protection of different and unequal faculties
of acquiring property, the possession of different degrees and kinds

of property immediately results; and from the influence of these on the sentiments and views of the respective proprietors, ensues a division of the society into different interests and parties.

The latent causes of faction are thus sown in the nature of man; and we see them everywhere brought into different degrees of activity, according to the different circumstances of civil society. A zeal for different opinions concerning religion, concerning government, and many other points, as well of speculation as of practice; an attachment to different leaders ambitiously contending for pre-eminence and power; or to persons of other descriptions whose fortunes have been interesting to the human passions, have, in turn, divided mankind into parties, inflamed them with mutual animosity, and rendered them much more disposed to vex and oppress each other than to co-operate for their common good. So strong is this propensity of mankind to fall into mutual animosities, that where no substantial occasion presents itself, the most frivolous and fanciful distinctions have been sufficient to kindle their unfriendly passions and excite their most violent conflicts. But the most common and durable source of factions has been the various and unequal distribution of property. Those who hold and those who are without property have ever formed distinct interests in society. Those who are creditors, and those who are debtors, fall under a like discrimination. A landed interest, a manufacturing interest, a mercantile interest, a moneyed interest, with many lesser interests, grow up of necessity in civilized nations, and divide them into different classes, actuated by different sentiments and views. The regulation of these various and interfering interests forms the principal task of modern legislation, and involves the spirit of party and faction in the necessary and ordinary operations of the government.

No man is allowed to be a judge in his own cause, because his interest would certainly bias his judgment, and, not improbably, corrupt his integrity. With equal, nay with greater reason, a body of men are unfit to be both judges and parties at the same time; yet what are many of the most important acts of legislation, but so many judicial determinations, not indeed concerning the rights of single persons, but concerning the rights of large bodies of citizens? And what are the different classes of legislators but advocates and parties to the causes which they determine? Is a law proposed concerning private debts? It is a question to which the creditors are parties on one side and the debtors on the other. Justice ought to hold the balance between them. Yet the parties are, and must be, themselves the judges; and the most numerous party, or, in other words, the most powerful faction must be expected to prevail. Shall domestic manufactures be encouraged, and in what degree, by restrictions on foreign manufactures? are questions which would be differently decided by the landed and the manufacturing classes, and probably by neither with a sole regard to justice and the public good. The apportionment of taxes on the various descriptions of property is an act which seems to require the most exact impartiality; yet there is, perhaps, no legislative act in which greater opportunity and temptation are given to a predominant party to trample on the rules of justice. Every shilling with which they overburden the inferior number, is a shilling saved to their own pockets.

It is in vain to say that enlightened statesmen will be able to adjust these clashing interests, and render them all subservient to the public good. Enlightened statesmen will not always be at the helm. Nor, in many cases, can such an adjustment be made at all without taking into view indirect and remote considerations, which will rarely prevail over the immediate interest which one party may find in disregarding the rights of another or the good of the whole.

The inference to which we are brought is, that the *causes* of faction cannot be removed, and that relief is only to be sought in the means of controlling its *effects*.

If a faction consists of less than a majority, relief is supplied by the republican principle, which enables the majority to defeat its sinister views by regular vote. It may clog the administration, it may convulse the society; but it will be unable to execute and mask its violence under the forms of the Constitution. When a majority is included in a faction, the form of popular government, on the other hand, enables it to sacrifice to its ruling passion or interest both the public good and the rights of other citizens. To secure the public good and private rights against the danger of such a faction, and at the same time to preserve the spirit and the form of popular government, is then the great object to which our inquiries are directed. Let me add that it is the great desideratum by which this form of government can be rescued from the opprobrium under which it has so long labored, and be recommended to the esteem and adoption of mankind.

By what means is this object attainable? Evidently by one of two only. Either the existence of the same passion or interest in a majority at the same time must be prevented, or the majority, having such coexistent passion or interest, must be rendered, by their number and local situation, unable to concert and carry into effect schemes of oppression. If the impulse and the opportunity be suffered to coincide, we well know that neither moral nor religious motives can be relied on as an adequate control. They are not found to be such on the injustice and violence of individuals, and lose their efficacy in proportion to the number combined together, that is, in proportion as their efficacy becomes needful.

From this view of the subject it may be concluded that a pure democracy, by which I mean a society consisting of a small number of citizens, who assemble and administer the government in person, can admit of no cure for the mischiefs of faction. A common passion or interest will, in almost every case, be felt by a majority of the whole; a communication and concert result from the form of government itself; and there is nothing to check the inducements to sacrifice the weaker party or an obnoxious individual. Hence it is that such democracies have ever been spectacles of turbulence and contention; have ever been found incompatible with personal security or the rights of property; and have in general been as short in their lives as they have been violent in their deaths. Theoretic politicians, who have patronized this species of government, have erroneously supposed that by reducing mankind to a perfect equality in their political rights, they would, at the same time, be perfectly equalized and assimilated in their possessions, their opinions, and their passions.

A republic, by which I mean a government in which the scheme of representation takes place, opens a different prospect, and promises the cure for which we are seeking. Let us examine the points in which it varies from pure democracy, and we shall comprehend both the nature of the cure and the efficacy which it must derive from the Union.

The two great points of difference between a democracy and a republic are: first, the delegation of the government, in the latter, to a small number of citizens elected by the rest; secondly, the greater number of citizens, and greater sphere of country, over which the latter may be extended.

The effect of the first difference is, on the one hand, to refine and enlarge the public views, by passing them through the medium of a chosen body of citizens, whose wisdom may best discern the true interest of their country, and whose patriotism and love of justice will be least likely to sacrifice it to temporary or partial considerations. Under such a regulation, it may well happen that the public voice, pronounced by the representatives of the people, will be more consonant to the public good than if pronounced by the people themselves, convened for the purpose. On the other hand, the effect may be inverted. Men of factious tempers, of local prejudices, or of sinister designs, may, by intrigue, by corruption, or by other means, first obtain the suffrages, and then betray the interests, of the people. The question resulting is, whether small or extensive republics are more favorable to the election of proper guardians of the public weal; and it is clearly decided in favor of the latter by two obvious considerations:

In the first place, it is to be remarked that, however small the republic may be, the representatives must be raised to a certain number, in order to guard against the cabals of a few; and that, however large it may be, they must be limited to a certain number, in order to guard against the confusion of a multitude. Hence, the number of

representatives in the two cases not being in proportion to that of
the two constituents, and being proportionally greater in the small
republic, it follows that, if the proportion of fit characters be not less
in the large than in the small republic, the former will present a
greater option, and consequently a greater probability of a fit choice.

In the next place, as each representative will be chosen by a greater
number of citizens in the large than in the small republic, it will be
more difficult for unworthy candidates to practice with success the
vicious arts by which elections are too often carried; and the suffrages
of the people being more free, will be more likely to centre in men
who possess the most attractive merit and the most diffusive and established characters.

It must be confessed that in this, as in most other cases, there is
a mean, on both sides of which inconveniences will be found to lie.
By enlarging too much the number of electors, you render the representative too little acquainted with all their local circumstances
and lesser interests; as by reducing it too much, you render him un-
duly attached to these, and too little fit to comprehend and pursue
great and national objects. The federal Constitution forms a happy
combination in this respect; the great and aggregate interests being
referred to the national, the local and particular to the State legis-
latures.

The other point of difference is, the great number of citizens and
extent of territory which may be brought within the compass of republican than of democratic government; and it is this circumstance
principally which renders factious combinations less to be dreaded in
the former than in the latter. The smaller the society, the fewer probably will be the distinct parties and interests composing it, the fewer
the distinct parties and interests, the more frequently will a majority
be found of the same party; and the smaller the number of individuals
composing a majority, and the smaller the compass within which they
are placed, the more easily will they concert and execute their plans
of oppression. Extend the sphere, and you take in a greater variety
of parties and interests; you make it less probable that a majority
of the whole will have a common motive to invade the rights of other
citizens; or if such a common motive exists, it will be more difficult
for all who feel it to discover their own strength, and to act in unison
with each other. Besides other impedements, it may be remarked that,
where there is a consciousness of unjust or dishonorable purposes,
communication is always checked by distrust in proportion to the
number whose concurrence is necessary.

Hence, it clearly appears, that the same advantage which a republic
has over a democracy, in controlling the effects of faction, is enjoyed
by a large over a small republic,—is enjoyed by the Union over the
States composing it. Does the advantage consist in the substitution of

representatives whose enlightened views and virtuous sentiments render them superior to local prejudices and to schemes of injustice? It will not be denied that the representation of the Union will be most likely to possess these requisite endowments. Does it consist in the greater security afforded by a greater variety of parties, against the event of any one party being able to outnumber and oppress the rest? In an equal degree does the increased variety of parties comprised within the Union, increase this security. Does it, in fine, consist in the greater obstacles opposed to the concert and accomplishment of the secret wishes of an unjust and interested majority? Here, again, the extent of the Union gives it the most palpable advantage.

The influence of factious leaders may kindle a flame within their particular States, but will be unable to spread a general conflagration through the other States. A religious sect may degenerate into a political faction in a part of the Confederacy; but the variety of sects dispersed over the entire face of it must secure the national councils against any danger from that source. A rage for paper money, for an abolition of debts, for an equal division of property, or for any other improper or wicked project, will be less apt to pervade the whole body of the Union than a particular member of it; in the same proportion as such a malady is more likely to taint a particular county or district, than an entire State.

In the extent and proper structure of the Union, therefore, we behold a republican remedy for the diseases most incident to republican government. And according to the degree of pleasure and pride we feel in being republicans, ought to be our zeal in cherishing the spirit and supporting the character of Federalists.

PUBLIUS

JAMES MADISON
FIRST INAUGURAL ADDRESS
March 4, 1809

*In this address, Madison set forth the principles and
purposes which he hoped to bring with him into the
Presidency. His dedication to peace and neutrality was
foremost among these principles.*

Unwilling to depart from examples of the most revered authroity, I
avail myself of the occasion now presented to express the profound
impression made on me by the call of my country to the station to
the duties of which I am about to pledge myself by the most solemn
of sanctions. So distinguished a mark of confidence, proceeding from
the deliberate and tranquil suffrage of a free and virtuous nation,
would under any circumstances have commanded my gratitude and
devotion, as well as filled me with an awful sense of the trust to be
assumed. Under the various circumstances which give peculiar solemnity to the existing period, I feel that both the honor and the responsibility allotted to me are inexpressibly enhanced.

The present situation of the world is indeed without a parallel,
and that of our own country full of difficulties. The pressure of these,
too, is the more severely felt because they have fallen upon us at a
moment when the national prosperity being at a height not before
attained, the contrast resulting from the change has been rendered the
more striking. Under the benign influence of our republican institutions,
and the maintenance of peace with all nations whilst so many of them
were engaged in bloody and wasteful wars, the fruits of a just policy
were enjoyed in an unrivaled growth of our faculties and resources.
Proofs of this were seen in the improvements of agriculture, in the
successful enterprises of commerce, in the progress of manufactures
and useful arts, in the increase of the public revenue and the use
made of it in reducing the public debt, and in the valuable works
and establishments everywhere multiplying over the face of our
land.

It is a precious reflection that the transition from this prosperous
condition of our country to the scene which has for some time been
distressing us is not chargeable on any unwarrantable views, nor, as
I trust, on any involuntary errors in the public councils. Indulging no
passions which trespass on the rights or the repose of other nations,
it has been the true glory of the United States to cultivate peace by
observing justice, and to entitle themselves to the respect of the nations at war by fulfilling their neutral obligations with the most scrupulous impartiality. If there be candor in the world, the truth of these
assertions will not be questioned;posterity at least will do justice to
them.

This unexceptionable course could not avail against the injustice and violence of the belligerent powers. In their rage against each other, or impelled by more direct motives, principles of retaliation have been introduced equally contrary to universal reason and acknowledged law. How long their arbitrary edicts will be continued in spite of the demonstrations that not even a pretext for them has been given by the United States, and of the fair and liberal attempt to induce a revocation of them, can not be anticipated. Assuring myself that under every vicissitude the determined spirit and united councils of the nation will be safeguards to its honor and its essential interests, I repair to the post assigned me with no other discouragement than what springs from my own inadequacy to its high duties. If I do not sink under the weight of this deep conviction it is because I find some support in a consciousness of the purposes and a confidence in the principles which I bring with me into this arduous service.

To cherish peace and friendly intercourse with all nations having correspondent dispositions; to maintain sincere neutrality toward belligerent nations; to prefer in all cases amicable discussion and reasonable accomodation of differences to a decision of them by an appeal to arms; to exclude foreign intrigues and foreign partialities, so degrading to all countries and so baneful to free ones; to foster a spirit of independence too just to invade the rights of others; too proud to surrender our own, too liberal to indulge unworthy prejudices ourselves and too elevated not to look upon them in others; to hold the union of the States as the basis of their peace and happiness; to support the Constitution, which is the cement of the Union, as well in its limitations as in its authorities; to respect the rights and authorities reserved to the States and to the people as equally incorporated with and essential to the success of the general system; to avoid the slightest interference with the rights of conscience or the functions of religion, so wisely exempted from civil jurisdiction; to preserve in their full energy the other salutary provisions in behalf of private and personal rights, and of the freedom of the press; to observe economy in public expenditures; to liberate the public resources by an honorable discharge of the public debts; to keep within the requisite limits a standing military force, always remembering that an armed and trained militia is the firmest bulwark of republics—that without standing armies their liberty can never be in danger, nor with large ones safe; to promote by authorized means improvements friendly to agriculture, to manufactures, and to external as well as internal commerce; to favor in like manner the advancement of science and the diffusion of information as the best aliment to true liberty; to carry on the benevolent plans which have been so meritoriously applied to the conversion of our aboriginal neighbors from the degradation and wretchedness of savage life to a participation of the improvements of which the human mind and manners are susceptible in a civilized state—as far as sentiments and intentions such as these can aid the fulfillment of my duty, they will be a resource which can not fail me.

It is my good fortune, moreover, to have the path in which I am to tread lighted by examples of illustrious services successfully rendered in the most trying difficulties by those who have marched before me. Of those of my immediate predecessor it might least become me here to speak. I may, however, be pardoned for not suppressing the sympathy with which my heart is full in the rich reward he enjoys in the benedictions of a beloved country, gratefully bestowed for exalted talents zealously devoted through a long career to the advancement of its highest interest and happiness.

But the source to which I look for the aids which alone can supply my deficiencies is in the well-tried intelligence and virtue of my fellow-citizens, and in the counsels of those representing them in the other departments associated in the care of the national interests. In these my confidence will under every difficulty be best placed, next to that which we have all been encouraged to feel in the guardianship and guidance of that Almighty Being whose power regulates the destiny of nations, whose blessings have been so conspicuously dispensed to this rising Republic, and to whom we are bound to address our devout gratitude for the past, as well as our fervent supplications and best hopes for the future.

JAMES MADISON

PROCLAMATION ON THE ERSKINE AGREEMENT
April 19, 1809

Assuming that British Orders in Council were to be withdrawn on June 10, 1809, as promised by the British Minister, David Erskine, Madison announced that thereafter trade would be resumed with Great Britain. The Erskine Agreement was repudiated by Great Britain when word was finally received there.

Whereas it is provided by the eleventh section of the act of Congress entitled "An act to interdict the commercial intercourse between the United States and Great Britain and France and their dependencies, and for other purposes," that "in case either France or Great Britain shall so revoke or modify her edicts as that they shall cease to violate the neutral commerce of the United States" the President is authorized to declare the same by proclamation, after which the trade suspended by the said act and by an act laying an embargo on all ships and vessels in the ports and harbors of the United States and the several acts supplementary thereto may be renewed with the nation so doing; and

Whereas the Honorable David Montague Erskine, His Britannic Majesty's envoy extraordinary and minister plenipotentiary, has, by the order and in the name of his Sovereign, declared to this Government that the British orders in council of January and November, 1807, will have been withdrawn as respects the United States on the 10th day of June next:

Now, therefore, I, James Madison, President of the United States, do hereby proclaim that the orders in council aforesaid will have been withdrawn on the said 10th day of June next, after which day the trade of the United States with Great Britain, as suspended by the act of Congress above mentioned and an act laying an embargo on all ships and vessels in the ports and harbors of the United States and the several acts supplementary thereto, may be renewed.

Given under my hand and the seal of the United States at Washington, the 19th day of April, A. D. 1809, and of the Independence of the United States the thirty-third.

JAMES MADISON

SPECIAL SESSION MESSAGE
May 23, 1809

*Since Madison's inaugural address dealt chiefly in
generalities, this message served to bring Congress up
to date on current affairs. The message was, on the
whole, optimistic. England had made a favorable change
in its foreign policy towards the United States and it
was hoped that France would do likewise. The President had "under the existing aspect of affairs" ordered all gunboats laid up except at New Orleans and
had discharged 100,000 militiamen from readiness for
immediate service.*

Fellow-Citizens of the Senate and of the House of Representatives:
On this first occasion of meeting you it affords me much satisfaction to be able to communicate the commencement of a favorable
change in our foreign relations, the critical state of which induced a
session of Congress at this early period.

In consequence of the provisions of the act interdicting commercial
intercourse with Great Britain and France, our ministers at London
and Paris were without delay instructed to let it be understood by
the French and British Governments that the authority vested in the
Executive to renew commercial intercourse with their respective nations would be exercised in the case specified by that act.

The works of defense for our seaport towns and harbors have proceeded with as much activity as the season of the year and other circumstances would admit. It is necessary, however, to state that, the
appropriations hitherto made being found to be deficient, a further
provision will claim the early consideration of Congress.

The whole of the 8 per cent stock remaining due by the United
States, amounting to $5,300,000, had been reimbursed on the last day
of the year 1808; and on the 1st day of April last the sum in the
Treasury exceeded $9,500,000. This, together with the receipts of the
current year on account of former revenue bonds, will probably be nearly if not altogether sufficient to defray the expenses of the year. But
the suspension of exports and the consequent decrease of importations
during the last twelve months will necessarily cause a great diminution in the receipts of the year 1810. After that year, should our foreign
relations be undisturbed, the revenue will again be more than commensurate to all the expenditures.

Aware of the inconveniences of a protracted session at the present
season of the year, I forbear to call the attention of the Legislature

to any matters not particularly urgent. It remains, therefore, only to assure you of the fidelity and alacrity with which I shall cooperate for the welfare and happiness of our country, and to pray that it may experience a continuance of the divine blessings by which it has been so signally favored.

JAMES MADISON

JAMES MADISON
FIRST ANNUAL MESSAGE
November 29, 1809

*This message to Congress was largely taken up with
the worsening relations with Great Britain. The President reviewed the British government's disavowal of
the Erskine Agreement and questioned how much authority the new British Minister had.*

Fellow-Citizens of the Senate and of the House of Representatives:

At the period of our last meeting I had the satisfaction of com-
municating an adjustment with one of the principal belligerent nations,
highly important in itself, and still more so as presaging a more extended accommodation. It is with deep concern I am now to inform
you that the favorable prospect has been overclouded by a refusal of
the British Government to abide by the act of its minister plenipotentiary, and by its ensuing policy toward the United States as seen
through the communications of the minister sent to replace him.

Whatever pleas may be urged for a disavowal of engagements formed
be injured by so unforeseen an occurrence; and I rely on the regard of
gagements a mutual ratification is reserved, or where notice at the
time may have been given of a departure from instructions, or in
extraordinary cases essentially violating the principles of equity, a
disavowal could not have been apprehended in a case where no such
notice or violation existed, where no such ratification was reserved,
and more especially where, as is now in proof, an engagement to be
executed without any such ratification was contemplated by the instructions given, and where it had with good faith been carried into
immediate execution on the part of the United States.

These considerations not having restrained the British Government
from disavowing the arrangement by virtue of which its orders in
council were to be revoked, and the event authorizing the renewal of
commercial intercourse having thus not taken place, it necessarily became a question of equal urgency and importance whether the act prohibiting that intercourse was not to be considered as remaining in
legal force. This question being, after due deliberation, determined in
the affirmative, a proclamation to that effect was issued. It could
not but happen, however, that a return to this state of things from
that which had followed an execution of the arrangement by the
United States would involve difficulties. With a view to diminish
these as much as possible, the instructions from the Secretary of the
Treasury now laid before you were transmitted to the collectors of the
several ports. If in permitting British vessels to depart without giving
bonds not to proceed to their own ports it should appear that the
tenor of legal authority has not been strictly pursued, it is to be as-

cribed to the anxious desire which was felt that no individuals should be injured by so unforeseen an occurrence; and I rely on the regard of Congress for the equitable interests of our own citizens to adopt whatever further provisions may be found requisite for a general remission of penalties involuntarily incurred.

Soon after these instructions were dispatched it was found that the British Government, anticipating from early proceedings of Congress at their last session the state of our laws, which has had the effect of placing the two belligerent powers on a footing of equal restrictions, and relying on the conciliatory disposition of the United States, had transmitted to their legation here provisional instructions not only to offer satisfaction for the attack on the frigate *Chesapeake*, and to make known the determination of His Britannic Majesty to send an envoy extraordinary with powers to conclude a treaty on all the points between the two countries, but, moreover, to signify his willingness in the meantime to withdraw his orders in council, in the persuasion that the intercourse with Great Britain would be renewed on the part of the United States.

These steps of the British Government led to the correspondence and the proclamation now laid before you, by virtue of which the commerce between the two countries will be renewable after the 10th day of June next.

Whilst I take pleasure in doing justice to the councils of His Britannic Majesty, which, no longer adhering to the policy which made an abandonment by France of her decrees a prerequisite to a revocation of the British orders, have substituted the amicable course which has issued thus happily, I can not do less than refer to the proposal heretofore made on the part of the United States, embracing a like restoration of the suspended commerce, as a proof of the spirit of accommodation which has at no time been intermitted, and to the result which now calls for our congratulations, as corroborating the principles by which the public councils have been guided during a period of the most trying embarrassments.

The discontinuance of the British orders as they respect the United States having been thus arranged, a communication of the event has been forwarded in one of our public vessels to our minister plenipotentiary at Paris, with instructions to avail himself of the important addition thereby made to the considerations which press on the justice of the French Government a revocation of its decrees or such a modification of them as that they shall cease to violate the neutral commerce of the United States.

The revision of our commercial laws proper to adapt them to the arrangement which has taken place with Great Britain will doubtless engage the early attention of Congress. It will be worthy at the same time of their just and provident care to make such further alterations in the laws as will more especially protect and foster the several branches of manufacture which have been recently instituted or extended by the laudable exertions of our citizens.

Under the existing aspect of our affairs I have thought it not inconsistent with a just precaution to have the gunboats, with the exception of those at New Orleans, placed in a situation incurring no expense beyond that requisite for their preservation and conveniency for future service, and to have the crews of those at New Orleans reduced to the number required for their navigation and safety.

I have thought also that our citizens detached in quotas of militia amounting to 100,000 under the act of March, 1808, might not improperly be relieved from the state in which they were held for immediate service. A discharge of them has been accordingly directed.

The progress made in raising and organizing the additional military force, for which provision was made by the act of April, 1808, together with the disposition of the troops, will appear by a report which the Secretary of War is preparing, and which will be laid before you.

Of the additional frigates required by an act of the last session to be fitted for actual service, two are in readiness, one nearly so, and the fourth is expected to be ready in the month of July. A report which the Secretary of the Navy is preparing on the subject, to be laid before Congress, will shew at the same time the progress made in officering and manning these ships. It will shew also the degree in which the provisions of the act relating to the other public armed ships have been carried into execution.

It will rest with the judgment of Congress to decide how far the change in our external prospects may authorize any modifications of the laws relating to the army and navy establishments.

The recall of the disavowed minister having been followed by the appointment of a successor, hopes were indulged that the new mission would contribute to alleviate the disappointment which had been produced, and to remove the causes which had so long embarassed the good understanding of the two nations. It could not be doubted that it would at least be charged with conciliatory explanations of the step which had been taken and with proposals to be substituted for the rejected arrangement. Reasonable and universal as this expectation was, it also has not been fulfilled. From the first official disclosures of the new minister it was found that he had received no authority to enter into explanations relative to either branch of the arrangement disavowed nor any authority to substitute proposals as to that branch which concerned the British orders in council, and, finally, that his proposals with respect to the other branch, the attack on the frigate Chesapeake, were founded on a presumption repeatedly declared to be inadmissible by the United States, that the first step toward adjustment was due from them, the proposals at the same

time omitting even a reference to the officer answerable for the mu-
derous aggression, and asserting a claim not less contrary to the British laws and British practice than to the principles and obligations
of the United States.

The correspondence between the Department of State and this minister will show how unessentially the features presented in its commencement have been varied in its progress. It will show also that,forgetting
the respect due to all governments, he did not refrain from imputa-
tions on this, which required that no further communications should
be received from him. The necessity of this step will be made known
to His Britannic Majesty through the minister plenipotentiary of the
United States in London; and it would indicate a want of the confidence due to a Government which so well understands and exacts what
becomes foreign ministers near it not to infer that the misconduct of
its own representative will be· viewed in the same light in which it
has been regarded here. The British Government will learn at the
same time that a ready attention will be given to communications
through any channel which may be substituted. It will be happy if
the change in this respect should be accompanied by a favorable revision of the unfriendly policy which has been so long pursued toward
the United States.

With France, the other belligerent,whose trespasses on our commercial right have long been the subject· of our just remonstrances,
the posture of our relations does not correspond with the measures
taken on the part of the United States to effect a favorable change.
The result of the several communications made to her Government,
in pursuance of the authorities vested by Congress in the Executive,
is contained in the correspondence of our minister at Paris now laid
before you.

By some of the other belligerents,although professing just and amicable dispositions, injuries materially affecting our commerce have not
been duly controlled or repressed. In these cases the interpositions
deemed proper on our part have not been omitted. But it well deserves the consideration of the Legislature how far both the safety and
the honor of the American flag may be consulted, by adequate provisions against that collusive prostitution of it by individuals unworthy
of the American name which has so much favored the real or pretended suspicions under which the honest commerce of their fellow-
citizens has suffered.

In relation to the powers on the coast of Barbary, nothing has
occurred which is not of a nature rather to inspire confidence than
distrust as to the continuance of the existing amity. With our Indian neighbors, the just and benevolent system continued toward them
has also preserved peace, and is more and more advancing habits
favorable to their civilization and happiness.

From a statement which will be made by the Secretary of War it will be seen that the fortifications on our maritime frontier are in many of the ports completed, affording the defense which was contemplated, and that a further time will be required to render complete the works in the harbor of New York and in some other places. By the enlargement of the works and the employment of a greater number of hands at the public armories the supply of small arms of an improving quality appears to be annually increasing at a rate that, with those made on private contract, may be expected to go far toward providing for the public exigency.

The act of Congress providing for the equipment of our vessels of war having been fully carried into execution, I refer to the statement of the Secretary of the Navy for the information which may be proper on that subject. To that statement is added a view of the transfers of appropriations authorized by the act of the session preceding the last and of the grounds on which the transfers were made.

Whatever may be the course of your deliberations on the subject of our military establishments, I should fail in my duty in not recommending to your serious attention the importance of giving to our militia, the great bulwark of our security and resource of our power, an organization the best adapted to eventual situations for which the United States ought to be prepared.

The sums which had been previously accumulated in the Treasury, together with the receipts during the year ending on the 30th of September last (and amounting to more than $9,000,000), have enabled us to fulfill all our engagements and to defray the current expenses of Government without recurring to any loan. But the insecurity of our commerce and the consequent diminution of the public revenue will probably produce a deficiency in the receipts of the ensuing year, for which and for other details I refer to the statements which will be transmitted from the Treasury.

In the state which has been presented of our affairs with the great parties to a disastrous and protracted war, carried on in a mode equally injurious and unjust to the United States as a neutral nation, the wisdom of the National Legislature will be again summoned to the important decision on the alternatives before them. That these will be met in a spirit worthy the councils of a nation conscious both of its rectitude and of its rights, and careful as well of its honor as of its peace, I have an entire confidence; and that the result will be stamped by a unanimity becoming the occasion, and be supported by every portion of our citizens with a patriotism enlightened and invigorated by experience, ought as little to be doubted.

In the midst of the wrongs and vexations experienced from external causes there is much room for congratulation on the prosperity and happiness flowing from our situation at home. The blessing of health has never been more universal. The fruits of the seasons, though in particular articles and districts short of their usual redundancy, are more than sufficient for our wants and our comforts. The fact of our country everywhere presents the evidence of laudable enterprise, of extensive capital, and of durable improvement. In a cultivation of the material and, the extension of useful manufactures, more especially in the general application to household fabrics, we behold a rapid diminution of our dependence on foreign supplies. Nor is it unworthy of reflection that this revolution in our pursuits and habits is in no slight degree a consequence of those impolitic and arbitrary edicts by which the contending nations, in endeavoring each of them to obstruct our trade with the other, have so far abridged our means of procuring the productions and manufactures of which our own are now taking the place.

Recollecting always that for every advantage which may contribute to distinguish our lot from that to which others are doomed by the unhappy spirit of the times we are indebted to that Divine Providence whose goodness has been so remarkably extended to this rissing nation, it becomes us to cherish a devout gratitude, and to implore from the same omnipotent source a blessing on the consultations and measures about to be undertaken for the welfare of our beloved country.

JAMES MADISON.

WEST FLORIDA PROCLAMATION
October 27, 1810

In this proclamation, Madison directed territorial officials to take possession of West Florida Legal justification for this action existed in a treaty of 1803 which gave title to the territory to the United States. Two weeks earlier an irregular army of Americans had seized West Florida from the Spanish and had thereupon declared itstelf to be a free and independent state.

Whereas the territory south of the Mississippi Territory and eastward of the river Mississippi, and extending to the river Perdido, of which possession was not delivered to the United States in pursuance of the treaty concluded at Paris on the 30th April, 1803, has at all times, as is well known, been considered and claimed by them as being within the colony of Louisiana conveyed by the said treaty in the same extent that it had in the hands of Spain and that it had when France originally possessed it; and

Whereas the acquiescence of the United States in the temporary continuance of the said territory under the Spanish authority was not the result of any distrust of their title, as had been particularly evinced by the general tenor of their laws and by the distinction made in the application of those laws between that territory and foreign countries, but was occasioned by their conciliatory views and by a confidence in the justice of their cause and in the success of candid discussion and amicable negotiation with a just and friendly power; and

Whereas a satisfactory adjustment, too long delayed, without the fault of the United States, has for some time been entirely suspended by events over which they had no control; and

Whereas a crisis has at length arrived subversive of the order of things under the Spanish authorities, whereby a failure of the United States to take the said territory into its possession may lead to events ultimately contravening the views of both parties, whilst in the meantime the tranquility and security of our adjourning territories are endangered and new facilities given to violations of our revenue and commerical laws and of those prohibiting the introduction of slaves;

Considering, moreover, that under these peculiar and imperative circumstances a forbearance on the part of the United States to occupy the territory in question, and thereby guard against the confusions and contingencies which threaten it, might be construed into a dereliction of their title or an insensibility to the importance of the stake; considering that in the hands of the United States it will not cease to be a subject of fair and friendly negotiation and adjustment; considering, finally, that the acts of Congress, though contemplating a present possession by a foreign authority, have contemplated also an eventual possession of the said territory by the United States, and are accordingly so framed as in that case to extend in ther operation to the same:

Now be it known that I, James Madison, President of the United States of America, in pursuance of these weighty and urgent considerations, have deemed it right and requisite that possessions should be taken of the said territory in the name and behalf of the United States. William C. C. Claiborne, governor of the Orleans Territory, of which the said Territory is to be taken as part, will accordingly proceed to execute the same and to exercise over the said Territory the authorities and functions legally appertaining to his office; and the good people inhabiting the same are invited and enjoined to pay due respect to him in that character, to be obedient to the laws, to maintain order, to cherish harmony, and in every manner to conduct themselves as peaceable citizens, under full assurance that they will be protected in the enjoyment of their liberty, property, and religion.

In testimony whereof I have caused the seal of the United to be hereunto affixed, and signed the same with my hand.

Done at the city of Washington, the 27th day of October, A. D. 1810, and in the thirty-fifth year of the Independence of the said United States.

JAMES MADISON.

REVIVAL OF NON—INTERCOURSE ACT AGAINST ENGLAND
November 2, 1810

The Macon Bill stipulated that should either France or England repeal its edicts or orders against American shipping, the Non-Intercourse Act of 1809 would be revived against the other nation within three months unless that nation revoked its restrictive measures. Since France announced the repeal of the Berlin and Milan decrees on August 5, pressure was put upon Great Britain to renounce her Orders in Council. In this proclamation, Madison served notice upon England.

Whereas by the fourth section of the act of Congress passed on the 1st day of May, 1810, entitled "An act concerning the commercial intercourse between the United States and Great Britain and France and their dependencies, and for other purposes," it is provided "that in case either Great Britain or France shall before the 3rd day of March next so revoke or modify her edicts as that they shall cease to violate the neutral commerce of the United States, which fact the President of the United States shall declare by proclamation, and if the other nation shall not within three months thereafter so revoke or modify her edicts in like manner, then the third, fourth, fifth, sixth, seventh, eighth, ninth, tenth, and eighteenth sections of the act entitled 'An act to interdict the commercial intercourse between the United States and Great Britain and France and their dependencies, and for other purposes,' shall from and after the expiration of three months from the date of the proclamation aforesaid be revived and have full force and effect so far as relates to the dominions, colonies, and dependencies, and to the articles the growth, produce, or manufacture of the dominions, colonies, and dependencies, of the nation thus refusing or neglecting to revoke or modify her edicts in the manner aforesaid. And the restrictions imposed by this act shall, from the date of such proclamation cease and be discontinued in relation to the nation revoking or modifying her decrees in the manner aforesaid;" and

Whereas it has been officially made known to this Government that the edicts of France violating the neutral commerce of the United States have been so revoked as to cease to have effect on the 1st of the present month:

Now, therefore, I, James Madison, President of the United States, do hereby proclaim that the said edicts of France have been so revoked as that they ceased on the said 1st day of the present month to violate the neutral commerce of the United States, and that from the date of these presents all the restrictions imposed by the aforesaid act shall cease and be discontinued in relation to France and their dependencies.

In testimony whereof I have caused the seal of the United States to be hereunto affixed, and signed the same with my hand, at the city of Washington, this 2d day of November, A. D. 1810, and of the Independence of the United States the thirty-fifth.

JAMES MADISON.

SECOND ANNUAL MESSAGE
December 5, 1810

Madison dealt with a wide range of problems in this message—from West Florida to the ever present difficulties caused by the British Orders in Council. One of Madison's more interesting points is buried towards the end of the message: a short paragraph (beginning "Among the commercial abuses still committed under the American flag. . . .") which denounces the slave trade as being in violation of the laws of humanity and which asks Congress to devise means of suppressing the evil.

Fellow-Citizens of the Senate and of the House of Representatives:

The embarrassments which have prevailed in our foreign relations, and so much employed the deliberations of Congress, make it a primary duty in meeting you to communicate whatever may have occurred in that branch of our national affairs.

The act of the last session of Congress concerning the commercial intercourse between the United States and Great Britain and France and their dependencies having invited in a new form a termination of their edicts against our neutral commerce, copies of the act were immediately forwarded to our ministers at London and Paris, with a view that its object might be within the early attention of the French and British Governments.

By the communication received through our minister at Paris it appeared that a knowledge of the act by the French Government was followed by a declaration that the Berlin and Milan decrees were revoked, and would cease to have effect on the 1st day of November ensuing. These being the only known edicts of France within the description of the act, and the revocation of them being such that they ceased at that date to violate our neutral commerce, the fact, as prescribed by law, was announced by a proclamation bearing the date the 2d day of November.

It would have well accorded with the conciliatory views indicated by this proceeding on the part of France to have extended them to all the grounds of just complaint which now remain unadjusted with the United States. It was particularly anticipated that, as a further evidence of just dispositions toward them, restoration would have been immediately made of the property of our citizens seized under a misapplication of the principle of reprisals combined with a misconstruction of a law of the United States. This expectation has not been fulfilled.

From the British Government no communication on the subject of the act has been received. To a communication from our minister at London of a revocation by the French Government of its Berlin and Milan decrees it was answered that the British system would be relinquished as soon as the repeal of the French decrees should have actually taken effect and the commerce of neutral nations have been restored to the condition in which it stood previously to the promulgation of those decrees. This pledge, although it does not necessarily import, does not exclude the intention of relinquishing, along with the orders in council the practice of those novel blockades which have a like effect of interrupting our neutral commerce, and this further justice to the United States is the rather to be looked for, inasmuch as the blockades in question, being not more contrary to the established law of nations than inconsistent with the rules of blockade formally recognized by Great Britain herself, could have no alleged basis other than the plea of retaliation alleged as the basis of the orders in council. Under the modification of the original orders of November, 1807, into the orders of April, 1809, there is, indeed, scarcely a nominal distinction between the orders and the blockades. One of those illegitimate blockades, bearing date in May, 1806, having been expressly avowed to be still unrescinded, and to be in effect comprehended in the orders in council, was too distinctly brought within the purview of the act of Congress not to be comprehended in the explanation of the requisites to a compliance with it. The British Government was accordingly apprised by our minister near it that such was the light in which the subject was to be regarded.

On the other important subjects depending between the United States and that Government no progress has been made from which an early and satisfactory result can be relied on.

In this new posture of our relations with those powers the consideration of Congress will be properly turned to a removal of doubts which may occur in the exposition and of difficulties in the execution of the act above cited.

The commerce of the United States with the north of Europe, heretofore much vexed by licentious cruisers, particularly under the Danish flag, has latterly been visited with fresh and extensive depredations. The measures pursued in behalf of our injured citizens not having obtained justice for them, a further and more formal interposition with the Danish Government is contemplated. The principles which have been maintained by that Government in relation to neutral commerce, and the friendly professions of His Danish Majesty toward the United States, are valuable pledges in favor of a successful issue.

Among the events growing out of the state of the Spanish Monarchy, our attention was imperiously attracted to the change developing itself in that portion of West Florida which, though of right appertaining to the United States, had remained in the possession of

Spain awaiting the result of negotiations for its actual delivery to them. The Spanish authority was subverted and a situation produced exposing the country to ulterior events which might essentially affect the rights and welfare of the Union. In such a conjuncture I did not delay the interposition required for the occupancy of the territory west of the river Perdido, to which the title of the United States extends,and to which the laws provided for the Territory of Orleans are applicable. With this view, the proclamation of which a copy is laid before you was confided to the governor of that Territory to be carried into effect. The legality and necessity of the course pursued assure me of the favorable light in which it will present itself to the Legislature, and of the promptitude with which they will supply whatever provisions may be due to the essential rights and equitable interests of the people thus brought into the bosom of the American family.

Our amity with the powers of Barbary, with the exception of a recent occurrence at Tunis, of which an explanation is just received, appears to have been uninterrupted and to have become more firmly established.

With the Indian tribes also the peace and friendship of the United States are found to be so eligible that the general disposition to preserve both continues to gain strength.

I feel particular satisfaction in remarking that an interior view of our country presents us with grateful proofs of its substantial and increasing prosperity. To a thriving agriculture and the improvements related to it is added a highly interesting extension of useful manufactures, the combined product of professional occupations and of household industry. Such indeed it the experience of economy as well as of policy in these substitutes for supplies heretofore obtained by foreign commerce that in a national view the change is justly regarded as of itself more than a recompense for those privations and losses resulting from foreign injustice which furnished the general impulse required for its accomplishment. How far it may be expedient to guard the infancy of this improvement in the distribution of labor by regulations of the commercial tariff is a subject which can not fail to suggest itself to your patriotic reflections.

It will rest with the consideration of Congress also whether a provident as well as fair encouragement would not be given to our navigation by such regulations as would place it on a level of competition with foreign vessels, particularly in transporting the important and bulky productions of our soil. The failure of equality and reciprocity in the existing regulations on this subject operates in our ports as a premium to foreign competitors, and the inconvenience must increase as these may be multiplied under more favorable circumstances by the more than countervailing encouragements now given them by the laws of their respective countries.

Whilst it is universally admitted that a well-instructed people alone can be permanently a free people, and whilst it is evident that the means of diffusing and improving useful knowledge form so small a proportion of the expenditures for national purposes, I can not presume it be to unseasonable to invite your attention to the advantages of superadding to the means of education provided by the several States a seminary of learning instituted by the National Legislature within the limits of their exclusive jurisdiction, the expense of which might be defrayed or reimbursed out of the vacant grounds which have accrued to the nation within those limits.

Such an institution, though local in its legal character, would be universal in its beneficial effects. By enlightening the opinions, by expanding the patriotism, and by assimilating the principles, the sentiments, and the manners of those who might resort to this temple of science, to be redistributed in due time through every part of the community, sources of jealousy and prejudice would be diminished, the features of national character would be multiplied, and greater extent given to social harmony. But, above all, a well-constituted seminary in the center of the nation is recommended by the consideration that the additional instruction emanating from it would contribute not less to strengthen the foundations than to adorn the structure of our free and happy system of government.

Among the commercial abuses still committed under the American flag, and leaving in force my former reference to that subject, it appears that American citizens are instrumental in carrying on a traffic in enslaved Africans, equally in violation of the laws of humanity and in defiance of those of their own country. The same just and benevolent motives which produced the interdiction in force against this criminal conduct will doubtless be felt by Congress in devising further means of suppressing the evil.

In the midst of uncertainties necessarily connected with the great interests of the United States, prudence requires a continuance of our defensive and precautionary arrangement. The Secretary of War and Secretary of the Navy will submit the statements and estimates which may aid Congress in their ensuring provisions for the land and naval forces. The statements of the latter will include a view of the transfer of appropriations in the naval expenditures and the grounds on which they were made.

The fortifications for the defense of our maritime frontier have been prosecuted according to the plan laid down in 1808. The works, with some exceptions, are completed and furnished with ordnance. Those for the security of the city of New York, though far advanced toward completion, will require a further time and appropriation. This is the case with a few others, either not completed or in need of repairs.

The improvements in quality and quantity made in the manufacture of cannon and small arms, both at the public armories and private factories, warrant additional confidence in the competency of these resources for supplying the public exigencies.

These preparations for arming the militia having thus far provided for one of the objects contemplated by the power vested in Congress with respect to that great bulwark of the public safety,it is for their consideration whether further provisions are not requisite for the other contemplated objects of organization and discipline. To give to this great mass of physical and moral force the efficiency which it merits, and is capable of receiving, it is indispensable that they should be instructed and practiced in the rules by which they are to be governed. Toward an accomplishment of this important work I recommend for the consideration of Congress the expediency of instituting a system which shall in the first instance call into the field at the public expense and for a given time certain portions of the commissioned and noncommissioned officers. The instruction and discipline thus acquired would gradually diffuse through the entire body of the miltia that practical knowledge and promptitude for active service which are the great end to be pursued. Experience has left no doubt either of the necessity or of the efficacy of competent military skill in those portions of an army in fitting it for the final duties which it may have to perform.

The Corps of Engineers, with the Military Academy, are entitled to the early attention of Congress. The buildings at the seat fixed by law for the present Academy are so far in decay as not to afford the necessary accommodation. But a revision of the law is recommended, principally with a view to a more enlarged cultivation and diffusion of the advantages of such institutions, by providing professorships for all the necessary branches of military instruction, and by the establishment of an additional academy at the seat of Government or elsewhere. The means by which war, as well for defense as for offense, are now carried on render these schools of the more scientific operations an indispensable part of every adequate system. Even among nations whose large standing armies and frequent wars afford every other opportunity of instruction these establishments are found to be indispensable for the due attainment of the branches of military science which require a regular course of study and experiment. In a government happily without the other opportunities seminaries where the elementary principles of the art of war can be taught without actual war, and without the expense of extensive and standing armies, have the precious advantage of uniting an essential preparation against external danger with a scrupulous regard to internal safety. In no other way, probably, can a provision of equal efficacy for the public defense be made at so little expense or more consistently with the public liberty.

The receipts into the Treasury during the year ending on the 30th of September last (and amounting to more than $8,500,000) have exceeded the current expenses of the Government, including the interest on the public debt. For the purpose of reimbursing at the end of the year $3,750,000 of the principal, a loan, as authorized by law, had been negotiated to that amount, but has since been reduced to $2,750,000, the reduction being permitted by the state of the Treasury, in which there will be a balance remaining at the end of the year estimated at $2,000,000. For the probable receipts of the next year and other details I refer to statements which will be transmitted from the Treasury, and which will enable you to judge what further provisions may be necessary for the ensuing years.

Reserving for future occasions in the course of the session whatever other communications may claim your attention, I close the present by expressing my reliance, under the blessing of Divine Providence, on the judgment and patriotism which will guide your measures at a period particularly calling for united councils and inflexible exertions for the welfare of our country, and by assuring you of the fidelity and alacrity with which my cooperation will be afforded.

JAMES MADISON.

JAMES MADISON
SECRET MESSAGE CONCERNING FLORIDA
January 3, 1811

In this secret message to Congress, Madison recommended a doctrine that foreshadowed the Monroe Doctrine.• Madison asked Congress to declare that the United States could not sit back and permit any part of a neighboring territory to pass from Spanish hands into those of another foreign power.

To the Senate and House of Representatives of the United States:

I communicate to Congress, in confidence, a letter of the 2d of December from Governor Folch, of West Florida, to the Secretary of State, and another of the same date from the same to John McKee.

I communicate in like manner a letter from the British charge d' affaires to the Secretary of State, with the answer of the latter. Although the letter can not have been written in consequence of any instruction from the British Government founded on the late order for taking possession of the portion of West Florida well known to be claimed by the United States; although no communication has ever been made by that Government to this of any stipulation with Spain in the present instance for the fulfillment of any such subsisting engagement, yet the spirit and scope of the document, with the accredited source from which it proceeds, required that it should not be withheld from the consideration of Congress.

Taking into view the tenor of these several communications, the posture of things with which they are connected, the intimate relation of the country adjoining the United States eastward of the river Perdido to their security and tranquillity, and the peculiar interest they otherwise have in its destiny, I recommend to the consideration of Congress the seasonableness of a declaration that the United States could not see without serious inquietude any part of a neighboring territory in which they have in different respects so deep and so just a concern pass from the hands of Spain into those of any other foreign power.

I recommend to their consideration also the expediency of authorizing the Executive to take temporary possession of any part or parts of the said Territory, in pursuance of arrangements which may be desired by the Spanish authorities, and for making provision for the government of the same during such possession.

The wisdom of Congress will at the same time determine how far it may be expedient to provide for the event of a subversion of the Spanish authorities within the Territory in question, and an apprehended occupancy thereof by any other foreign power.

JAMES MADISON.

VETO OF EPISCOPAL CHURCH BILL
February 21, 1811

*Madison had always been highly conscious of the sepa-
ration between church and state—more so than most
of his countrymen. Here, he vetoed a bill incorporating the Protestant Episcopal Church in the District
of Columbia on the constitutional grounds that "Congress shall make no law respecting a religious establishment."*

To the House of Representatives of the United States:

Having examined and considered the bill entitled "An act incorporating the Protestant Episcopal Church in the town of Alexandria,
in the District of Columbia," I now return the bill to the House of
Representatives, in which it originated, with the following objections:

Because the bill exceeds the rightful authority to which governments
are limited by the essential distinction between civil and religious
functions, and violates in particular the article of the Constitution of
the United States which declares that "Congress shall make no law
respecting a religious establishment." The bill enacts into and estab-
lishes by law sundry rules and proceedings relative purely to the organization and polity of the church incorporated, and comprehending
even the election and removal of the minister of the same, so that
no change could be made therein by the particular society or by the
general church of which it is a member, and whose authority it recog-
nizes. This particular church, therefore, would so far be a religious
establishment by law, a legal force and sanction being given to certain articles in its constitution and administration. Nor can it be considered that the articles thus established are to be taken as the des-
criptive criteria only of the corporate indentity of the society, inasmuch as this identity must depend on other characteristics, as the
regulations established are generally unessential and alterable according
to the principles and canons by which churches of that denomination
govern themselves, and as the injunctions and prohibitions contained
in the regulations would be enforced by the penal consequences applicable to a violation of them according to the local law.

Because the bill vests in the said incorporated church an authority
to provide for the support of the poor and the education of poor
children of the same, an authority which, being altogether superfluous
if the provision is to be the result of pious charity, would be a pre-
cedent for giving to religious societies as such a legal agency in carrying into effect a public and civil duty.

JAMES MADISON.

JAMES MADISON

THIRD ANNUAL MESSAGE
November 5, 1811

Although Madison included in this address a sharp criticism of France—calculated to silence the attacks of the Federalists—all of the measures proposed pointed toward war with England.

Fellow-Citizens of the Senate and of the House of Representatives:

In calling you together sooner than a separation from your homes would otherwise have been required I yielded to considerations drawn from the posture of our foreign affairs, and in fixing the present for the time of your meeting regard was had to the probability of further developments of the policy of the belligerent powers toward this country which might the more unite the national councils in the measures to be pursued.

At the close of the last session of Congress it was hoped that the successive confirmations of the extinction of the French decrees, so far as they violated our neutral commerce, would have induced the Government of Great Britain to repeal its orders in council, and thereby authorize a removal of the existing obstructions to her commerce with the United States.

Instead of this reasonable step toward satisfaction and friendship between the two nations, the orders were, at a moment when least to have been expected, put into more rigorous execution; and it was communicated through the British envoy just arrived that whilst the revocation of the edicts of France, as officially made known to the British Government, was denied to have taken place, it was an indispensable condition of the repeal of the British orders that commerce should be restored to a footing that would admit the productions and manufactures of Great Britain, when owned by neutrals, into markets shut against them by her enemy, the United States being given to understand that in the meantime a continuance of their nonimportation act would lead to measures of retaliation.

At a later date it has indeed appeared that a communication to the British Government of fresh evidence of the repeal of the French decrees against our neutral trade was followed by an intimation that it had been transmitted to the British plenipotentiary here in order that it might receive full consideration in the depending discussions. This communication appears not to have been received; but the transmission of it hither, instead of founding on it an actual repeal of the orders or assurances that the repeal would ensue, will not permit us to rely on any effective change in the British cabinet. To be ready to meet with cordiality satisfactory proofs of such a change, and to proceed in the meantime in adapting our measures to the views which have been disclosed through that minister will best consult our whole duty.

In the unfriendly spirit of those disclosures indemnity and redress for other wrongs have continued to be withheld, and our coasts and the mouths of our harbors have again witnessed scenes not less derogatory to the dearest of our national rights than vexations to the regular course of our trade.

Among the occurrences produced by the conduct of British ships of war hovering on our coast was an encounter between one of them and the American frigate commanded by Captain Rodgers, rendered unavoidable on the part of the latter by a fire commenced without cause by the former, whose commander is therefore alone chargeable with the blood unfortunately shed in maintaining the honor of the American flag. The proceedings of a court of inquiry requested by Captain Rodgers are communicated, together with the correspondence relating to the occurrence, between the Secretary of State and His Britannic Majesty's envoy. To these are added the several correspondences which have passed on the subject of the British orders in council, and to both the correspondence relating to the Floridas, in which Congress will be made acquainted with the interposition which the Government of Great Britain has thought proper to make against the proceeding of the United States.

The justice and fairness which have been evinced on the part of the United States toward France, both before and since the revocation of her decrees, authorized an expectation that her Government would have followed up that measure by all such others as were due to our reasonable claims, as well as dictated by its amicable professions. No proof, however, is yet given of an intention to repair the other wrongs done to the United States, and particularly to restore the great amount of American property seized and condemned under edicts which, though not affecting our neutral relations, and therefore not entering into questions between the United States and other belligerents, were nevertheless founded in such unjust principles that the reparation ought to have been prompt and ample.

In addition to this and other demands of strict right on that nation, the United States have much reason to be dissatisfied with the rigorous and unexpected restrictions to which their trade with the French dominions has been subjected, and which, if not discontinued, will require at least corresponding restrictions on importations from France into the United States.

On all those subjects our minister plenipotentiary lately sent to Paris has carried with him the necessary instructions, the result of which will be communicated to you, and, by ascertaining the ulterior policy of the French Government toward the United States, will enable you to adapt to it that of the United States toward France.

Our other foreign relations remain without unfavorable changes. With

Russia they are on the best footing of friendship. The ports of Sweden have afforded proofs of friendly dispositions toward our commerce in the councils of that nation also, and the information from our special minister to Denmark shews that the mission had been attended with valuable effects to our citizens, whose property had been so extensively violated and endangered by cruisers under the Danish flag.

Under the ominous indications which commanded attention it became a duty to exert the means committed to the executive department in providing for the general security. The works of defense on our maritime frontier have accordingly been prosecuted' with an activity leaving little to be added for the completion of the most important ones, and, as particularly suited for cooperation in emergencies, a portion of the gunboats have in particular harbors been ordered into use. The ships of war before in commission, with the addition of a frigate, have been chiefly employed as a cruising guard to the rights of our coast, and such a disposition has been made of our land forces as was thought to promise the services most appropriate and important. In this disposition is included a force consisting of regulars and militia, embodied in the Indiana Territory and marched toward our northwestern frontier. This measure was made requisite by several murders and depredations committed by Indians, but more especially by the meanacing preparations and aspect of a combination of them on the Wabash, under the influence and direction of a fanatic of the Shawanese tribe. With these exceptions the Indian tribes retain their peaceable dispositions toward us, and their usual pursuits.

I must now add that the period is arrived which claims from the legislative guardians of the national rights a system of more ample provisions for maintaining them. Notwithstanding the scrupulous justice, the protracted moderation, and the multiplied efforts on the part of the United States to substitute for the accumulating dangers to the peace of the two countries all the mutual advantages of reestablished friendship and confidence, we have seen that the British cabinet perseveres not only in withholding a remedy for other wrongs, so long and so loudly calling for it, but in the execution, brought home to the threshold of our territory, of measures which under existing circumstances have the character as well as the effect of war on our lawful commerce.

With this evidence of hostile inflexibility in trampling on rights which no independent nation can relinquish, Congress will feel the duty of putting the United States into an armor and an attitude demanded by the crisis, and corresponding with the national spirit and expectations.

I recommend, accordingly, that adequate provision be made for filling the ranks and prolonging the enlistments of the regular troops; for an auxiliary force to be engaged for a more limited term; for the acceptance of volunteer corps, whose patriotic ardor may court a participation in urgent services; for detachments as they may be wanted of other portions of the militia, and for such a preparation of the great body as will proportion its usefulness to its intrinsic capacities. Nor can the occasion fail to remind you of the importance of those military seminaries which in every event will form a valuable and frugal part of our military establishment.

The manufacture of cannon and small arms has proceeded with due success, and the stock and resources of all the necessary munitions are adequate to emergencies. It will not be inexpedient, however, for Congress to authorize an enlargement of them.

Your attention will of course be drawn to such provisions on the subject of our naval force as may be required for the services to which it may be best adapted. I submit to Congress the seasonableness also of an authority to augment the stock of such materials as are imperishable in their nature, or may not at once be attainable.

In contemplating the scenes which distinguish this momentous epoch, and estimating their claims to our attention, it is impossible to overlook those developing themselves among the great communities which occupy the southern portion of our own hemisphere and extend into our neighborhood. An enlarged philanthropy and an enlightened forecast concur in imposing on the national councils an obligation to take a deep interest in their destinies, to cherish reciprocal sentiments of good will, to regard the progress of events, and not to be unprepared for whatever order of things may be ultimately established.

Under another aspect of our situation the early attention of Congress will be due to the expediency of further guards against evasions and infractions of our commercial laws. The practice of smuggling, which is odious everywhere, and particularly criminal in free governments, where, the laws being made by all for the good of all, a fraud is committed on every individual as well as on the state, attains its utmost guilt when it blends with a pursuit of ignominious gain a treacherous subserviency, in the transgressors, to a foreign policy adverse to that of their own country. It is then that the virtuous indignation of the public should be enabled to manifest itself through the regular animadversions of the most competent laws.

To secure greater respect to our mercantile flag, and to the honest interest which it covers, it is expedient also that it be made punishable in our citizens to accept licenses from foreign governments for a trade unlawfully interdicted by them to other American citizens, or to trade under false colors or papers of any sort.

A prohibition is equally called for against the acceptance by our citizens of special licenses to be used in a trade with the United States, and against the admission into particular ports of the United States of vessels from foreign countries authorized to trade with particular ports only.

Although other subjects will press more immediately on your deliberations, a portion of them can not but be well bestowed on the just and sound policy of securing to our manufactures the success they have attained, and are still attaining, in some degree, under the impulse of causes not permanent, and to our navigation, the fair extent of which is at present abridged by the unequal regulations of foreign governments.

Besides the reasonableness of saving our manufactures from sacrifices which a change of circumstances might bring on them, the national interest requires that, with respect to such articles at least as belong to our defense and our primary wants, we should not be left in unnecessary dependence on external supplies. And whilst foreign governments adhere to the existing discriminations in their ports against our navigation, and an equality or lesser discrimination is enjoyed by their navigation in our ports, the effect can not be mistaken, because it has been seriously felt by our shipping interests; and in proportion as this takes place the advantages of an independent conveyance of our products to foreign markets and of a growing body of mariners trained by their occupations for the service of their country in times of danger must be diminished.

The receipts into the Treasury during the year ending on the 30th of September last have exceeded $13,500,000, and have enabled us to defray the current expenses, including the interest on the public debt, and to reimburse more than $5,000,000 of the principal without recurring to the loan authorized by the act of the last session. The temporary loan obtained in the latter end of the year 1810 has also been reimbursed, and is not included in that amount.

The decrease of revenue arising from the situation of our commerce, and the extraordinary expenses which have and may become necessary, must be taken into view in making commensurate provisions for the ensuing year; and I recommend to your consideration the propriety of insuring a sufficiency of annual revenue at least to defray the ordinary expenses of Government, and to pay the interest on the public debt, including that on new loans which may be authorized.

I can not close this communication without expressing my deep sense of the crisis in which you are assembled, my confidence in a wise and honorable result to your deliberations, and assurances of the faithful zeal with which my cooperating duties will be discharged, invoking at the same time the blessing of Heaven on our beloved country and on all the means that may be employed in vindicating its rights and advancing its welfare.

JAMES MADISON.

PRELUDE TO WAR
June 1, 1812

*With a declaration of war against Great Britain only
a little more than two weeks away, Madison sent this
message to Congress, reviewing relations between England and the United States. It is, naturally enough, a
document that paints Britain in the darkest colors
and justifies the declaration of war that America was
soon to make.*

To the Senate and House of Representatives of the United States:
I communicate to Congress certain documents, being a continuation of those heretofore laid before them on the subject of our affairs with Great Britain.

Without going back beyond the renewal in 1803 of the war in which
Great Britain is engaged, and omitting unrepaired wrongs of inferior
magnitude, the conduct of her Government presents a series of acts
hostile to the United States as an independent and neutral nation.

British cruisers have been in the continued practice of violating the
American flag on the great highway of nations, and of seizing and carrying off persons sailing under it, not in the exercise of a belligerent
right founded on the law of nations against an enemy, but of a municipal prerogative over British subjects. British jurisdiction is thus extended to neutral vessels in a situation where no laws can operate
but the law of nations and the laws of the country to which the vessels belong, and a self-redress is assumed which, if British subjects were
wrongfully detained and alone concerned, is that substitution of force
for a resort to the responsible sovereign which falls within the definition of war. Could the seizure of British subjects in such cases be regarded as within the exercise of a belligerent right, the acknowledged
laws of war, which forbid an article of captured property to be adjud-
ged without a regular investigation before a competent tribunal, would
imperiously demand the fairest trial where the sacred rights of persons
were at issue. In place of such a trial these rights are subjected to the
will of every petty commander.

The practice, hence, is so far from affecting British subjects alone
that, under the pretext of searching for these, thousands of American
citizens, under the safeguard of public law and of their national flag,
have been torn from their country and from everything dear to them;
have been dragged on board ships of war of a foreign nation and exposed, under the severities of their discipline, to be exiled to the most
distant and deadly climes, to risk their lives in the battles of their
oppressors, and to be the melancholy instruments of taking away those
of their own brethren.

Against this crying enormity, which Great Britain would be so prompt to avenge if committed against herself, the United States have in vain exhausted remonstrances and expostulations, and that no proof might be wanting of their conciliatory dispositions, and no pretext left for a continuance of the practice,the British Government was formally assured of the readiness of the United States to enter into arrangements such as could not be rejected if the recovery of British subjects were the real and the sole object. The communication passed without effect.

British cruisers have been in the practice also of violating the rights and the peace of our coasts. They hover over and harass our entering and departing commerce. To the most insulting pretensions they have added the most lawless proceedings in our very harbors, and have wantonly spilt American blood within the sanctuary of our territorial jurisdiction. The principles and rules enforced by that nation, when a neutral nation, against armed vessels of belligerents hovering near her coasts and disturbing her commerce are well known. When called on, nevertheless, by the United States to punish the greater offenses committed by her own vessels, her Government has bestowed on their commanders additional marks of honor and confidence.

Under pretended blockades, without the presence of an adequate force and sometimes without the practicability of applying one, our commerce has been plundered in every sea, the great staples of our country have been cut off from their legitimate markets, and a destructive blow aimed at our agricultural and maritime interests. In aggravation of these predatory measures they have been considered as in force from the dates of their notification, a retrospective effect being thus added, as has been done in other important cases, to the unlawfulness of the course pursued. And to render the outrage the more signal these mock blockades have been reiterated and enforced in the face of official communications from the British Government declaring as the true definition of a legal blockade "that particular ports must be actually invested and previous warning given to vessels bound to them not to enter."

Not content with these occasional expedients for laying waste our neutral trade, the cabinet of Britain resorted at length to the sweeping system of blockades, under the name of orders in council, which has been molded and managed as might best suit its political views, its commercial jealousies, or the avidity of British cruisers.

To our remonstrances against the complicated and transcendent injustice of this innovation the first reply was that the orders were reluctantly adopted by Great Britain as a necessary retaliation on decrees of her enemy proclaiming a general blockade of the British Isles at a time when the naval force of that enemy dared not issue from his own ports. She was reminded without effect that her own prior blockades, unsupported by an adequate naval force actually applied and continued, were a bar to this plea; that executed edicts against millions of our property could not be retaliation on edicts confessedly impossible to be executed; that retailiation, to be just, should fall on the party setting the guilty example, not on an innocent party which was not even chargeable with an acquiescence in it.

When deprived of this flimsy veil for a prohibition of our trade with her enemy by the repeal of his prohibition of our trade with Great Britain, her cabinet, instead of a corresponding repeal or a practical discontinuance of its orders, formally avowed a determination to persist in them against the United States until the markets of her enemy should be laid open to British products, thus asserting an obligation on a neutral power to require one belligerent to encourage by its internal regulations the trade of another belligerent, contradicting her own practice toward all nations, in peace as well as in war, and betraying the insincerity of those professions which inculcated a belief that, having restored to her orders with regret, she was anxious to find an occasion for putting an end to them.

Abandoning still more all respect for the neutral rights of the United States and for its own consistency, the British Government now demands as prerequisites to a repeal of its orders as they relate to the United States that a formality should be observed in the repeal of the French decrees nowise necessary to their termination nor exemplified by British usage, and that the French repeal, besides including that portion of the decrees which operates within a territorial jurisdiction, as well as that which operates on the high seas, against the commerce of the United States should not be a single and special repeal in relation to the United States, but should be extended to whatever other neutral nations unconnected with them may be affected by those decrees. And as an additional insult, they are called on for a formal disavowal of conditions and pretensions advanced by the French Government for which the United States are so far from having made themselves responsible that, in official explanations which have been published to the world, and in a correspondence of the American minister at London with the British minister for foreign affairs such a responsibility was explicitly and emphatically disclaimed.

It has become, indeed, sufficiently certain that the commerce of the United States is to be sacrificed, not as interfering with the belligerent rights of Great Britain; not as supplying the wants of her enemies, which she herself supplies; but as interfering with the monopoly which she covets for her own commerce and navigation. She carries on a war against the lawful commerce of a friend that she may the better carry on a commerce with an enemy—a commerce polluted by the forgeries and perjuries which are for the most part the only passports by which it can succeed.

Anxious to make every experiment short of the last resort of injured nations, the United States have withheld from Great Britain, under successive modifications, the benefits of a free intercourse with their market, the loss of which could not but outweigh the profits accruing from her restrictions of our commerce with other nations. And to entitle these experiments to the more favorable consideration they were so framed as toenable her to place her adversary under the exclusive operation of them. To these appeals her Government has been equally inflexible, as if willing to make sacrifices of every sort rather than yield to the claims of justice or renounce the errors of a false pride. Nay, so far were the attempts carried to overcome the attachment of the British cabinet to its unjust edicts that it received every encouragement within the competency of the executive branch of our Government to expect that a repeal of them would be followed by a war between the United States and France, unless the French edicts should also be repealed. Even this communication, although silencing forever the plea of a disposition in the United States to acquiesce in those edicts originally the sole plea for them, received no attention.

If no other proof existed of a predetermination of the British Government against a repeal of its orders, it might be found in the correspondence of the minister plenipotentiary of the United States at London and the British secretary for foreign affairs in 1810, on the question whether the blockade of May, 1806, was considered as in force or as not in force. It had been ascertained that the French Government, which urged this blockade as the ground of its Berlin decree,was willing in the event of its removal to repeal that decree, which, being followed by alternate repeals of the other offensive edicts, might abolish the whole system on both sides. This inviting opportunity for accomplishing an object so important to the United States, and professed so often to be the desire of both the belligerents, was made known to the British Government. As that Government admist that an actual application of an adequate force is necessary to the existence of a legal blockade, and it was notorious that if such a force had ever been applied its long discontinuance had annulled the blockade in question, there could be no sufficient objection on the part of Great Britain to a formal revocation of it, and no imaginable objection to a declaration of the fact that the blockade did not exist. The declaration would have been consistent with her avowed principles of blockade, and would have enabled the United States to demand from France the pledged repeal of her decrees, either with success, in which case the way would have been opened for a general repeal of the belligerent edicts, or without success, in which case the United States would have been justified in turning their measures exclusively against France. The British Government would, however, neither rescind the blockade nor declare its nonexistence, nor permit its nonexistence to be inferred and affirmed by the American plenipotentiary. On the contrary, by representing the blockade to be comprehended in the orders in council, the United States were compelled so to regard it in their subsequent proceedings.

There was a period when a favorable change in the policy of the British cabinet was justly considered as established. The minister plenipotentiary of His Britannic Majesty here proposed an adjustment of the differences more immediately endangering the harmony of the two countries. The proposition was accepted with the promptitude and cordiality corresponding with the invariable professions of this Government. A foundation appeared to be laid for a sincere and lasting reconciliation. The prospect, however, quickly vanished. The whole proceeding was disavowed by the British Government without any explanations which could at that time repress the belief that the disavowal proceeded from a spirit of hostility to the commercial rights and prosperity of the United States; and it has since come into proof that at the very moment when the public minister was holding the language of friendship and inspiring confidence in the sincerity of the negotiation with which he was charged a secret agent of his Government was employed in intrigues having for their object a subversion of our Government and a dismemberment of our happy union.

In reviewing the conduct of Great Britain toward the United States our attention is necessarily drawn to the warfare just renewed by the savages on one of our extensive frontiers—a warfare which is known to spare neither age nor sex and to be distinguished by features peculiarly shocking to humanity. It is difficult to account for the activity and combinations which have for some time been developing themselves among tribes in constant intercourse with British traders and garrisons without connecting their hostility with that influence and without recollecting the authenticated examples of such interpositions heretofore furnished by the officers and agents of that Government.

Such is the spectacle of injuries and indignities which have been heaped on our country, and such the crisis which its unexampled forbearance and conciliatory efforts have not been able to avert. It might at least have been expected that an enlightened nation, if less urged by moral obligations or invited by friendly dispositions on the part of the United States, would have found in its true interest alone a sufficient motive to respect their rights and their tranquillity on the high seas; that an enlarged policy would have favored that free and general circulation of commerce in which the British nation is at all times interested, and which in times of war is the best alleviation of its calamities to herself as well as to other belligerents;and more especially that the British cabinet would not, for the sake of a precarious and surreptitious intercourse with hostile markets, have perservered in a course of measures which necessarily put at hazard the invaluable market of a great and growing country, disposed to cultivate the mutual advantages of an active commerce.

Other counsels have prevailed. Our moderation and conciliation have had no other effect than to encourage perserverance and to enlarge pretensions. We behold our seafaring citizens still the daily victims of lawless violence, committed on the great common and highway of nations, even within sight of the country which owes them protection. We behold our vessels, freighted with the products of our soil and industry, or returning with the honest proceeds of them, wrested from their lawful destinations, confiscated by prize courts no longer the organs of public law but the instruments of arbitrary edicts, and their unfortunate crews dispersed and lost, or forced or inveigled in British ports into British fleets, whilst arguments are employed in support of these aggressions which have no foundation but in a principle equally supporting a claim to regulate our external commerce in all cases whatsoever.

We behold, in fine, on the side of Great Britain a state of war against the United States, and on the side of the United States a state of peace toward Great Britain.

Whether the United States shall continue passive under these progressive usurpations and these accumulating wrongs, or, opposing force to force in defense of their national rights, shall commit a just cause into the hands of the Almighty Disposer of Events, avoiding all connections which might entangle it in the contest or views of other powers, and preserving a constant readiness to concur in an honorable reestablishment of peace and friendship, is a solemn question which the Constitution wisely confides to the legislative department of the Government. In recommending it to their early deliberations I am happy in the assurance that the decision will be worthy the enlightened and patriotic councils of a virtuous, a free, and a powerful nation.

Having presented this view of the relations of the United States with Great Britain and of the solemn alternative growing out of them, I proceed to remark that the communications last made to Congress on the subject of our relations with France will have shewn that since the revocation of her decrees, as they violated the neutral rights of the United States, her Government has authorized illegal captures by its privateers and public ships, and that other outrages have been practiced on our vessels and our citizens. It will have been seen also that no indemnity had been provided or satisfactorily pledged for the extensive spoliations committed under the violent and retrospective orders of the French Government against the property of our citizens seized within the jurisdiction of France. I abstain at this time from recommending to the consideration of Congress definitive measures with respect to that nation, in the expectation that the result of unclosed discussions between our minister plenipotentiary at Paris and the French Government will speedily enable Congress to decide with greater advantage on the course due to the rights, the interests, and the honor of our country.

JAMES MADISON.

JAMES MADISON

PUBLIC HUMILIATION AND PRAYER
July 9, 1812

A firm believer in the separation of church and state, Madison was very much against official appeals to God for such blessings as victory and prosperity. The pressures of Congress and the public were nevertheless strong enough at times to force him to issue proclamations such as the one below. In this proclamation, notice how Madison disassociates himself from all religious aspects; Congress is designated as the body desiring a proclamation and religious denominations so disposed will be enabled to offer prayers.

Whereas the Congress of the United States, by a joint resolution of the two Houses, have signified a request that a day may be recommended to be observed by the people of the United States with religious solemnity as a day of public humiliation and prayer; and

Whereas such a recommendation will enable the several religious denominations and societies so disposed to offer at one and the same time their common vows and adorations to Almighty God on the solemn occasion produced by the war in which He has been pleased to permit the injustice of a foreign power to involve these United States:

I do therefore recommend the third Thursday in August next as a convenient day to be set apart for the devout purposes of rendering the Sovereign of the Universe and the Benefactor of Mankind the public homage due to His holy attributes; of acknowledging the transgressions which might justly provoke the manifestations of His divine displeasure; of seeking His merciful forgiveness and His assistance in the great duties of repentance and amendment, and especially of offering fervent supplications that in the present season of calamity and war He would take the American people under His peculiar care and protection; that He would guide their public councils, animate their patriotism, and bestow His blessing on their arms; that He would inspire all nations with a love of justice and of concord and with a reverence for the unerring precept of our holy religion to do to others as they would require that others should do to them; and, finally, that, turning the hearts of our enemies from the violence and injustice which sway their councils against us, He would hasten a restoration of the blessings of peace.

Given at Washington, the 9th day of July, A. D. 1812.

JAMES MADISON.

FOURTH ANNUAL MESSAGE
November 4, 1812

*Among the topics covered in this first wartime an-
nual message were the surrender of Detroit by General
Hull, the refusal of the Governors of Massachussetts
and Connecticut to furnish the required militias for
coastal defense and the need for stronger laws to prevent merchant ships from sailing under British licenses.*

Fellow-Citizens of the Senate and of the House of Representatives:
On our present meeting it is my first duty to invite your attention
to the providential favors which our country has experienced in the
unusual degree of health dispensed to its inhabitants, and in the rich
abundance with which the earth has rewarded the labors bestowed
on it. In the successful cultivation of other branches of industry, and
in the progress of general improvement favorable to the national prosperity, there is just occasion also for our mutual congratulations and
thankfulness.

With these blessings are necessarily mingled the pressures and vicissitudes incident to the state of war into which the United States have
been forced by the perserverance of a foreign power in its system of
injustice and aggression.

Previous to its declaration it was deemed proper, as a measure of
precaution and forecast, that a considerable force should be placed in
the Michigan Territory with a general view to its security, and, in
the event of war, to such operations in the uppermost Canada as
would intercept the hostile influence of Great Britain over the savages,
obtain the command of the lake on which that part of Canada borders,
and maintain cooperating relations with such forces as might be most
conveniently employed against other parts. Brigadier-General Hull
was charged with this provisional service, having under his command a
body of troops composed of regulars and of volunteers from the State
of Ohio. Having reached his destination after his knowledge of the
war, and possessing discretionary authority to act offensively , he
passed into the neighboring territory of the enemy with a prospect
of easy and victorious progress. The expedition, nevertheless, terminated unfortunately, not only in a retreat to the town and fort of
Detroit, but in the surrender of both and of the gallant corps commanded by that officer. The causes of this painful reverse will be in-
vestigated by a military tribunal.

A distinguishing feature in the operations which preceded and followed this adverse event is the use made by the enemy of the merciless savages under their influence. Whilst the benevolent policy of the

United States invariably recommended peace and promoted civilization among that wretched portion of the human race, and was making exertions to dissuade them from taking either side in the war, the enemy has not scrupled to call to his aid their ruthless ferocity, armed with the horrors of those instruments of carnage and torture which are known to spare neither age nor sex. In this outrage against the laws of honorable war and against the feelings sacred to humanity the British commanders can not resort to a plea of retaliation, for it is committed in the face of our example. They can not mitigate it by calling it a self-defense against men in arms, for it embraces the most shocking butcheries of defenseless families. Nor can it be pretended that they are not answerable for the atrocities perpetrated, since the savages are employed with a knowledge, and even with menaces, that their fury could not be controlled. Such is the spectacle which the deputed authorities of a nation boasting its religion and morality have not been restrained from presenting to an enlightened age.

The misfortune at Detroit was not, however, without a consoling effect. It was followed by signal proofs that the national spirit rises according to the pressure on it. The loss of an important post and of the brave men surrendered with it inspired everywhere new ardor and determination. In the States and districts least remote it was no sooner known than every citizen was ready to fly with his arms at once to protect his brethren against the bloodthirsty savages let loose by the enemy on an extensive frontier, and to convert a partial calamity into a source of invigorated efforts. This patriotic zeal, which it was necessary rather to limit than excite, has embodied an ample force from States of Kentucky and Ohio and from parts of Pennsylvania and Virginia. It is placed, with the addition of a few regulars, under the command of Brigadier-General Harrison, who possesses the entire confidence of his fellow-soldiers, among whom are citizens, some of them volunteers in the ranks, not less distinguished by their political stations than by their personal merits. The greater portion of this force is proceeding on its destination toward the Michigan Territory, having succeeded in relieving an important frontier post, and in several incidental operations against hostile tribes of savages, rendered indispensable by the subserviency into which they had been seduced by the enemy—a seduction the more cruel as it could not fail to impose a necessity of precautionary severities against those who yielded to it.

At a recent date an attack was made on a post of the enemy near Niagara by a detachment of the regular and other forces under the command of Major-General Van Rensselaer, of the militia of the State of New York. The attack, it appears, was ordered in compliance with the ardor of the troops, who executed it with distinguished gallantry, and were for a time victorious; but not receiving the expected support, they were compelled to yield to reinforcements of British regulars and savages. Our loss has been considerable, and is deeply to be lamented. That of the enemy, less ascertained, will be the more felt, as it includes among the killed the commanding general, who was also the governor of the Province, and was sustained by veteran troops from unexperienced soldiers, who must daily improve in the duties of the field.

Our expectation of gaining the command of the Lakes by the invasion of Canada from Detroit having been disappointed, measures were instantly taken to provide them a naval force superior to that of the enemy. From the talents and activity of the officer charged with this object everything that can be done may be expected. Should the present season not admit of complete success, the progress made will insure for the next a naval ascendency where it is essential to our permanent peace with and control over the savages.

Among the incidents to the measures of the war I am constrained to advert to the refusal of the governors of Massachusetts and Connecticut to furnish the required detachments of militia toward the defense of the maritime frontier. The refusal was founded on a novel and unfortunate exposition of the provisions of the Constitution relating to the militia. The correspondences which will be laid before you contain the requisite information on the subject. It is obvious that if the authority of the United States to call into service and command the militia for the public defense can be thus frustrated, even in a state of declared war and of course under apprehensions of invasion preceding war, they are not one nation for the purpose most of all requiring it, and that the public safety may have no other resource than in those large and permanent military establishments which are forbidden by the principles of our free government, and against the necessity of which the militia were meant to be a constitutional bulwark.

On the coasts and on the ocean the war has been as successful as circumstances inseparable from its early stages could promise. Our public ships and private cruisers, by their activity, and, where there was occasion, by their intrepidity, have made the enemy sensible of the difference between a reciprocity of captures and the long confinement of them to their side. Our trade, with little exception, has safely reached our ports, having been much favored in it by the course pursued by a squadron of our frigates under the command of Commodore Rodgers, and in the instance in which skill and bravery were more particularly tried with those of the enemy the American flag had an auspicious triumph. The frigate Constitution, commanded by Captain Hull, after a close and short engagement completely disabled and captured a British frigate, gaining for that officer and all on board a praise which can not be too liberally bestowed, not merely for the victory actually achieved, but for that prompt and cool exertion of commanding talents which, giving to courage its highest character, and to the force applied its full effect, proved that more could have been done in a contest requiring more.

Anxious to abridge the evils from which a state of war can not be exempt, I lost no time after it was declared in conveying to the British Government the terms on which its progress might be arrested, without awaiting the delays of a formal and final pacification, and our charge d'affaires at London was at the same time authorized to agree to an armistice founded upon them. These terms required that the orders in council should be repealed as they affected the United States, without a revival of blockades violating acknowledged rules, and that there should be an immediate discharge of American seamen from British ships, and a stop to impressment from American ships, with an understanding that an exclusion of the seamen of each nation from the ships of the other should be stipulated, and that the armistice should be improved into a definitive and comprehensive adjustment of depending controversies. Although a repeal of the orders susceptible of explanations meeting the views of this Government had taken place before this pacific advance was communicated to that of Great Britain, the advance was declined from an avowed repugnance to a suspension of the practice of impressments during the armistice, and without any intimation that the arrangement proposed with respect to seamen would be accepted. Whether the subsequent communications from this Government, affording an occasion for reconsidering the subject on the part of Great Britain, will be viewed in a more favorable light or received in a more accommodating spirit remains to be known. It would be unwise to relax our measures in any respect on a presumption of such a result.

The documents from the Department of State which relate to this subject will give a view also of the propositions for an armistice which have been received here, one of them from the authorities at Halifax and in Canada, the other from the British Government itself through Admiral Warren, and of the grounds on which neither of them could be accepted.

Our affairs with France retain the posture which they held at my last communications to you. Notwithstanding the authorized expectations of an early as well as favorable issue to the discussions on foot, these have been procrastinated to the latest date. The only intervening occurrence meriting attention is the promulgation of a French decree purporting to be a definitive repeal of the Berlin and Milan decrees. This proceeding, although made the ground of the repeal of the British orders in council, is rendered by the time and manner of it liable to many objections.

The final communications from our special minister to Denmark afford further proofs of the good effects of his mission, and of the amicable disposition of the Danish Government. From Russia we have the satisfaction to receive assurances of continued friendship, and that it will not be affected by the rupture between the United States and Great Britain. Sweden also professes sentiments favorable to the subsisting harmony.

With the Barbary Powers, excepting that of Algiers, our affairs remain on the ordinary footing. The consul-general residing with that Regency has suddenly and without cause been banished, together with all the American citizens found there. Whether this was the transitory effect of capricious despotism or the first act of predetermined hostility is not ascertained. Precautions were taken by the consul on the latter supposition.

The Indian tribes not under foreign instigations remain at peace, and receive the civilizing attentions which have proved so beneficial to them.

With a view to that vigorous prosecution of the war to which our national faculties are adequate, the attention of Congress will be particularly drawn to the insufficiency of existing provisions for filling up the military establishment. Such is the happy condition of our country, arising from the facility of subsistence and the high wages for every species of occupation, that notwithstanding the augmented inducements provided at the last session, a partial success only has attended the recruiting service. The deficiency has been necessarily supplied during the campaign by other than regular troops, with all the inconveniences and expense incident to them. The remedy lies in establishing more favorably for the private soldier the proportion between his recompense and the term of his enlistment, and it is a subject which can not too soon or too seriously be taken into consideration.

The same insufficiency has been experienced in the provisions for volunteers made by an act of the last session. The recompense for the service required in this case is still less attractive than in the other, and although patriotism alone has sent into the field some valuable corps of that description, those alone who can afford the sacrifice can be reasonably expected to yield to that impulse.

It will merit consideration also whether as auxiliary to the security of our frontiers corps may not be advantageously organized with a restriction of their services to particular districts convenient to them, and whether the local and occasional services of mariners and others in the seaport towns under a similar organization would not be a provident addition to the means of their defense.

I recommend a provision for an increase of the general officers of the Army, the deficiency of which has been illustrated by the number and distance of separate commands which the course of the war and the advantage of the service have required.

And I can not press too strongly on the earliest attention of the

Legislature the importance of the reorganization of the staff establishment with a view to render more distinct and definite the relations and responsibilities of its several departments. That there is room for improvements which will materially promote both economy and success in what appertains to the Army and the war is equally inculcated by the examples of other countries and by the experience of our own.

A revision of the militia laws for the purpose of rendering them more systematic and better adapting them to emergencies of the war is at this time particularly desirable.

Of the additional ships authorized to be fitted for service, two will be shortly ready to sail, a third is under repair, and delay will be avoided in the repair of the residue. Of the appropriations for the purchase of materials for shipbuilding, the greater part has been applied to that object and the purchase will be continued with the balance.

The enterprising spirit which has characterized our naval force and its success, both in restraining insults and depredations on our coasts and in reprisals on the enemy, will not fail to recommend an enlargement of it.

There being reason to believe that the act prohibiting the acceptance of British licenses is not a sufficient guard against the use of them, for purposes favorable to the interests and views of the enemy, further provisions on that subject are highly important. Nor is it less so that penal enactments should be provided for cases of corrupt and perfidious intercourse with the enemy, not amounting to treason nor yet embraced by any statutory provisions.

A considerable number of American vessels which were in England when the revocation of the orders in council took place were laden with British manufactures under an erroneous impression that the nonimportation act would immediately cease to operate, and have arrived in the United States. It did not appear proper to exercise on unforeseen cases of such magnitude the ordinary powers vested in the Treasury Department to mitigate forfeitures without previously affording to Congress an opportunity of making on the subject such provision as they may think proper. In their decision they will doubtless equally consult what is due to equitable considerations and to the public interest.

The receipts into the Treasury during the year ending on the 30th of September last have exceeded $16,500,000 which have been sufficient to defray all the demands on the Treasury to that day, including a necessary reimbursement of near three millions of the principal of the public debt. In these receipts is included a sum of near $5,850,000, received on account of the loans authorized by the acts of the last session; the whole sum actually obtained on loan amounts to $11,000,-000, the residue of which, being receivable subsequent to the 30th of

September last, will, together with the current revenue, enable us to defray all the expenses of this year.

The duties on the late unexpected importations of British manufactures will render the revenue of the ensuing year more productive than could have been anticipated.

The situation of our country, fellow-citizens, is not without its difficulties, though it abounds in animating considerations, of which the view here presented of our pecuniary resources is an example. With more than one nation we have serious and unsettled controversies, and with one, powerful in the means and habits of war, we are at war. The spirit and strength of the nation are nevertheless equal to the support of all its rights, and to carry it through all its trials. They can be met in that confidence. Above all, we have the inestimable consolation of knowing that the war in which we are actually engaged is a war neither of ambition nor of vainglory; that it is waged not in violation of the rights of others, but in the maintenance of our own; that it was preceded by a patience without example under wrongs accumulating without end, and that it was finally not declared until every hope of·averting it was extinguished by the transfer of the British scepter into new hands clinging to former councils, and until declarations were reiterated to the last hour, through the British envoy here, that the hostile edicts against our commerical rights and our maritime independence would not be revoked; nay, that they could not be revoked without violating the obligations of Great Britain to other powers, as well as to her own interests. To have shrunk under such circumstances from manly resistance would have been a degradation blasting our best and proudest hopes; it would have struck us from the high rank where the virtuous struggles of our fathers had placed us, and have betrayed the magnificènt legacy which we hold in trust for future generations. It would have acknowledged that on the element which forms three-fourths of the globe we inhabit, and where all independent nations have equal and common rights, the American people were not an independent people, but colonists and vassals. It was at this moment and with such an alternative that war was chosen. The nation felt the necessity of it, and called for it. The appeal was accordingly made, in a just cause, to the Just and All-powerful Being who holds in His hand the chain of events and the destiny of nations. It remains only that, faithful to ourselves, entangled in no connections with the views of other powers, and ever ready to accept peace from the hand of justice, we prosecute the war with united counsels and with the ample faculties of the nation until peace be so obtained and as the only means under the Divine blessing of speedily obtaining it.

JAMES MADISON.

SECOND INAUGURAL ADDRESS
March 4, 1813

Madison used this occasion to justify the United States purpose and conduct in the war. At the same time, he castigated British actions, particularly the employment of Indians.

About to add the solemnity of an oath to the obligations imposed by a second call to the station in which my country heretofore placed me, I find in the presence of this respectable assembly an opportunity of publicly repeating my profound sense of so distinguished a confidence and of the responsibility united with it. The impressions on me are strengthened by such an evidence that my faithful endeavors to discharge my arduous duties have been favorably estimated, and by a consideration of the momentous period at which the trust has been renewed. From the weight and magnitude now belonging to it I should be compelled to shrink if I had less reliance on the support of an enlightened and generous people, and felt less deeply a conviction that the war with a powerful nation, which forms so prominent a feature in our situation, is stamped with that justice which invites the smiles of Heaven on the means of conducting it to a successful termination.

May we not cherish this sentiment without presumption when we reflect on the characters by which this war is distinguished?

It was not declared on the part of the United States until it had been long made on them, in reality though not in name; until arguments and expostulations had been exhausted; until a positive declaration had been received that the wrongs provoking it would not be discontinued; nor until this last appeal could no longer by delayed without breaking down the spirit of the nation, destroying all confidence in itself and in its political institutions, and either perpetuating a state of disgraceful suffering or regaining by more costly sacrifices and more severe struggles our lost rank and respect among independent powers.

On the issue of the war are staked our national sovereignty on the high seas and the security of an important class of citizens, whose occupations give the proper value to those of every other class. Not to contend for such a stake is to surrender our equality with other powers on the element common to all and to violate the sacred title which every member of the society has to its protection. I need not call into view the unlawfulness of the practice by which our mariners are forced at the will of every cruising officer from their own vessels into foreign ones, nor paint the outrages inseparable from it. The proofs are in the records of each successive Administration of our Government, and the cruel sufferings of that portion of the American people have found their way to every bosom not dead to the sympathies of human nature.

As the war was just in its origin and necessary and noble in its objects, we can reflect with a proud satisfaction that in carrying it on no principle of justice or honor, no usage of civilized nations, no precept of courtesy or humanity, have been infringed. The war has been waged on our part with scrupulous regard to all these obligations, and in a spirit of liberality which was never surpassed.

How little has been the effect of this example on the conduct of the enemy!

They have retained as prisoners of war citizens of the United States not liable to be so considered under the usages of war.

They have refused to consider as prisoners of war, and threatened to punish as traitors and deserters, persons emigrating without restraint to the United States, incorporated by naturalization into our political family, and fighting under the authority of their adopted country in open and honorable war for the maintenance of its rights and safety. Such is the avowed purpose of the Government which is in the practice of naturalizing by thousands citizens of other countries, and not only of permitting but compelling them to fight its battles against their native country.

They have not, it is true, taken into their own hands the hatchet and the knife, devoted to indiscriminate massacre, but they have let loose the savages armed with these cruel instruments; have allured them into their service, and carried them to battle by their sides, eager to glut their savage thirst with the blood of the vanquished and to finish the work of torture and death on maimed and defenseless captives. And, what was never before seen, British commanders have extorted victory over the unconquerable valor of our troops by presenting to the sympathy of their chief captives awaiting massacre from their savage associates. And now we find them, in further contempt of the modes of honorable warfare, supplying the place of a conquering force by attempts to disorganize our political society, to dismember our confederated Republic. Happily, like others, these will recoil on the authors; but they mark the degenerate counsels from which they emanate, and if they did not belong to a series of unexampled inconsistencies might excite the greater wonder as proceeding from a Government which founded the very war in which it has been so long engaged on a charge against the disorganizing and insurrectional policy of its adversary.

To render the justice of the war on our part the more conspicuous, the reluctance to commence it was followed by the earliest and strongest manifestations of a disposition to arrest its progress. The sword was scarcely out of the scabbard before the enemy was apprised of the reasonable terms on which it would be resheathed. Still more precise advances were repeated, and have been received in a spirit forbidding every reliance not placed on the military resources of the nation.

These resources are amply sufficient to bring the war to an honorable issue. Our nation is in number more than half that of the British Isles. It is composed of a brave, a free, a virtuous, and an intelligent people. Our country abounds in the necessaries, the arts, and the comforts of life. A general prosperity is visible in the public countenance. The means employed by the British cabinet to undermine it have recoiled on themselves; have given to our national faculties a more rapid development, and, draining or diverting the precious metals from British circulation and British vaults, have poured them into those of the United States. It is a propitious consideration that an unavoidable war should have found this seasonable facility for the contributions required to support it. When the public voice called for war, all knew, and still know, that without them it could not be carried on through the period which it might last, and the patriotism, the good sense, and the manly spirit of our fellow-citizens are pledges for the cheerfulness with which they will bear each his share of the common burden. To render the war short and its success sure, animated and systematic exertions alone are necessary, and the success of our arms now may long preserve our country from the necessity of another resort to them. Already have the gallant exploits of our naval heroes proved to the world our inherent capacity to maintain our rights on one element. If the reputation of our arms has been thrown under clouds on the other, presaging flashes of heroic enterprise assure us that nothing is wanting to correspondent triumphs there also but the discipline and habits which are in daily progress.

SPECIAL SESSION MESSAGE
May 25, 1813

Although Madison covered many topics in this ad-
dress—the appointment of peaçe commissioners in re-
sponse to the Russian mediation proposal, the im-
pressment of seamen and the conduct of the war on
land and sea—the nation fixed its attention on the
President's call for additional taxes. The Federalist
papers, in particular, were bitter in their criticism.
One sore point with Republicans and Federalists alike
was that Secretary of the Treasury Gallatin had left
on the peace mission. Many people felt that he had
"run away" after advocating increased taxes.

Fellow-Citizens of the Senate and of the House of Representatives:

At an early day after the close of the last session of Congress an offer was formally communicated from His Imperial Majesty the Emperor of Russia of his mediation, as the common friend of the United States and Great Britain, for the purpose of facilitating a peace between them. The high character of the Emperor Alexander being a satisfactory pledge for the sincerity and impartiality of his offer, it was immediately accepted, and as a further proof of the disposition on the part of the United States to meet their adversary in honorable experiments for terminating the war it was determined to avoid intermediate delays incident to the distance of the parties by a definitive provision for the contemplated negotiation. Three of our eminent citizens were accordingly commissioned with the requisite powers to conclude a treaty of peace with persons clothed with like powers on the part of Great Britain. They are authorized also to enter into such conventional regulations of the commerce between the two countries as may be mutually advantageous. The two envoys who where in the United States at the time of their appointment have proceeded to join their colleague already at St. Petersburg.

The envoys have received another commission authorizing them to conclude with Russia a treaty of commerce with a view to strengthen the amicable relations and improve the beneficial intercourse between the two countries.

The issue of this friendly interposition of the Russian Emperor and this pacific manifestation on the part of the United States time only can decide. That the sentiments of Great Britain toward that Sovereign will have produced an acceptance of .his offered mediation must be presumed. That no adequate motives exist to prefer a continuance of war with the United States to the terms on which they are willing to close it is certain. The British cabinet also must be sensible that, with respect to the important question of impressment, on which the war so essentially turns, a search for or seizure of British persons or property on board neutral vessels on the high seas is not a belligerent right derived from the law of nations, and it is obvious that no visit or search or use of force for any purpose on board the vessels of one independent power on the high seas can in war or peace be sanctioned by the laws or authority of another power. It is equally obvious that, for the purpose of preserving to each State its seafaring members, by excluding them from the vessels of the other, the mode heretofore proposed by the United States and now enacted by them as an article of municipal policy, can not for a moment be compared with the mode practiced by Great Britain without a conviction of its title to preference, inasmuch as the latter leaves the discrimination between the mariners of the two nations to officers exposed by unavoidable bias as well as by a defect of evidence to a wrong decision, under circumstances precluding for the most part the enforcement of controlling penalties, and where a wrong decision, besides the irreparable violation of the sacred rights of persons, might frustrate the plans and profits of entire voyages; whereas the mode assumed by the United States guards with studied fairness and efficacy against errors in such cases and avoids the effect of casual errors on the safety of navigation and the success of mercantile expeditions.

If the reasonableness of expectations drawn from these considerations could guarantee their fulfillment a just peace would not be distant. But it becomes the wisdom of the National Legislature to keep in mind the true policy, or rather the indispensable obligation, of adapting its measures to the supposition that the only course to that happy event is in the vigorous employment of the resources of war. And painful as the reflection is, this duty is particularly enforced by the spirit and manner in which the war continues to be waged by the enemy, who, uninfluenced by the unvaried examples of humanity set them, are adding to the savage fury of it on one frontier a system of plunder and conflagration on the other, equally forbidden by respect for national character and by the established rules of civilized warfare.

As an encouragement to persevering and invigorated exertions to bring the contest to a happy result, I have the satisfaction of being able to appeal to the auspicious progress of our arms both by land and on the water.

In continuation of the brilliant achievements of our infant Navy, a signal triumph has been gained by Captain Lawrence and his companions in the *Hornet* sloop of war, which destroyed a British sloop of war with a celerity so unexampled and with a slaughter of the enemy so disproportionate to the loss in the *Hornet* as to claim for the conquerors the highest praise and the full recompense provided by Congress in preceding cases. Our public ships of war in general, as well as the private armed vessels, have continued also their activity and success against the commerce of the enemy, and by their vigilance and address have greatly frustrated the efforts of the hostile squadrons distributed along our coasts to intercept them in returning into port and resuming their cruises.

The augmentation of our naval force, as authorized at the last session of Congress, is in progress. On the Lakes our superiority is near at hand where it is not already established.

The events of the campaign, so far as they are known to us, furnish matter of congratulation, and show that under a wise organization and efficient direction the Army is destined to a glory not less brilliant than that which already encircles the Navy. The attack and capture of York is in that quarter a presage of future and greater victories, while on the western frontier the issue of the late siege of Fort Meigs leaves us nothing to regret but a single act of inconsiderate valor.

The provisions last made for filling the ranks and enlarging the staff of the Army have had the best effects. It will be for the consideration of Congress whether other provisions depending on their authority may not still further improve the military establishment and the means of defense.

The sudden death of the distinguished citizen who represented the United States in France, without any special arrangements by him for such a contingency, has left us without the expected sequel to his last communications, nor has the French Government taken any measures for bringing the depending negotiations to a conclusion through its representative in the United States. This failure adds to delays before so unreasonably spun out. A successor to our deceased minister has been appointed and is ready to proceed on his mission. The course which he will pursue in fulfilling it is that prescribed by a steady regard to the true interests of the United States, which equally avoids an abandonment of their just demands and a connection of their fortunes with the systems of other powers.

The receipts in the Treasury from the 1st of October to the 31st day of March last, including the sums received on account of Treasury notes and of the loans authorized by the acts of the last and the preceding sessions of Congress, have amounted to $15,412,000. The expenditures during the same period amounted to $15,920,000, and left in the Treasury on the 1st of April the sum of $1,857,000. The loan of $16,000,000, authorized by the act of the 8th of February last, has been contracted for. Of that sum more than $1,000,000 had been paid into the Treasury prior to the 1st of April, and formed a part of the receipts as above stated. The remainder of that loan, amounting to near $15,000,000, with the sum of $5,000,000 authorized to be issued in Treasury notes, and the estimated receipts from the customs and the sales of public lands, amounting to $9,300,000, and making, in the whole, $29,300,000, to be received during the last nine months of the present year, will be necessary to meet the expenditures already authorized and the engagements contracted in relation to the public debt. These engagements amount during that period to $10,500,000, which, with near one million for the civil, miscellaneous, and diplomatic expenses, both foreign and domestic, and $17,800,000 for the military and naval expenditures, including the ships of war building and to be built, will leave a sum in the Treasury at the end of the present year equal to that on the 1st of April last. A part of this sum may be considered as a resource for defraying any extraordinary expenses already authorized by law beyond the sums above estimated, and a further resource for any emergency may be found in the sum of $1,000,-000, the loan of which to the United States has been authorized by the State of Pennsylvania, but which has not yet been brought into effect.

This view of our finances, whilst it shows that due provision has been made for the expenses of the current year, shows at the same time, by the limited amount of the actual revenue and the dependence on loans, the necessity of providing more adequately for the future supplies of the Treasury. This can be best done by a well-digested system of internal revenue in aid of existing sources, which will have the effect both of abridging the amount of necessary loans and, on that account, as well as by placing the public credit on a more satisfactory basis, of improving the terms on which loans may be obtained. The loan of sixteen millions was not contracted for at a less interest than about 7 1/2 per cent, and, although other causes may have had an agency, it can not be doubted that, with the advantage of a more extended and less precarious revenue, a lower rate of interest might have sufficed. A longer postponement of this advantage could not fail to have a still greater influence on future loans.

In recommending to the National Legislature this resort to additional taxes I feel great satisfaction in the assurance that our constituents, who have already displayed so much zeal and firmess in the cause of their country, will cheerfully give any other proof of their patriotism which it calls for. Happily no people, with local and transitory exceptions never to be wholly avoided, are more able than the people of the United States to spare for the public wants a portion of their private means, whether regard be had to the ordinary profits of industry or the ordinary price of subsistence in our country compared with those in any other. And in no case could stronger reasons be felt for yielding the requisite contributions. By rendering the public resources certain and commensurate to the public exigencies, the constituted authorities will be able to prosecute the war the more rapidly to its proper issue; every hostile hope founded on a calculated failure of our resources will be cut off, and by adding to the evidence of bravery and skill in combats on the ocean and the land, and alacrity in supplying the treasure necessary to give them their fullest effect, and demonstrating to the world the public energy which our political institutions combine, with the personal liberty distinguishing them, the best security will be provided against future enterprises on the rights or the peace of the nation.

The contest in which the United States are engaged appeals for its support to every motive that can animate an uncorrupted and enlightened people—to the love of country; to the pride of liberty; to an emulation of the glorious founders of their independence by a successful vindication of its violated attributes; to the gratitude and sympathy which demand security from the most degrading wrongs of a class of citizens who have proved themselves so worthy the protection of their country by their heroic zeal in its defense; and, finally, to the sacred obligation of transmitting entire to future generations that precious patrimony of national rights and independence which is held in trust by the present from the goodness of Divine Providence.

Being aware of the inconveniences to which a protracted session at this season would be liable, I limit the present communication to objects of primary importance. In special messages which may ensue regard will be had to the same consideration.

JAMES MADISON.

FIFTH ANNUAL MESSAGE
December 7, 1813

*The end of the year 1813 found the United States
with more successes than failures in its prosecution
of the war, Madison said in this address. But of the
paramount question of the day — the peace mission —
Madison had heard nothing. It was known, however,
that the British had declined the Russian offer of
mediation and Madison wondered whether the British
were guilty of "mistaking our desire for peace for
a dread of British power."*

Fellow-Citizens of the Senate and of the House of Respresentatives:

In meeting you at the present interesting conjuncture it would have
been highly satisfactory if I could have communicated a favorable
result to the mission charged with negotiations for restoring peace.
It was a just expectation, from the respect due to the distinguished
Sovereign who had invited them by his offer of mediatior., from the
readiness with which the invitation was accepted on the part of the
United States, and from the pledge to be found in an act of their
Legislature for the liberality which their plenipotentiaries would carry
into the negotiations, that no time would be lost by the British Government in embracing the experiment for hastening a stop to the
effusion of blood. A prompt and cordial acceptance of the mediation
on that side was the less to be doubted, as it was of a nature not
to submit rights or pretensions on either side to the decision of an
umpire, but to afford merely an opportunity, honorable and desirable
to both, for discussing and, if possible, adjusting them for the interest of both.

The British cabinet, either mistaking our desire of peace for a dread
of British power or misled by other fallacious calculations, has disappointed this reasonable anticipation. No communications from our envoys having reached us, no information on the subject has been received from that source; but it is known that the mediation was declined in the first instance, and there is no evidence, notwithstanding
the lapse of time, that a change of disposition in the British councils has taken place or is to be expected.

Under such circumstances a nation proud of its rights and conscious of its strength has no choice but an exertion of the one in
support of the other.

To this determination the best encouragement is derived from the
success with which it has pleased the Almighty to bless our arms
both on the land and on the water.

Whilst proofs have been continued of the enterprise and skill of our cruisers, public and private, on the ocean, and a new trophy gained in the capture of a British by an American vessel of war, after an action giving celebrity to the name of the victorious commander, the great inland waters on which the enemy were also to be encountered have presented achievements of our naval arms as brilliant in their character as they have been important in their consequences.

On Lake Erie, the squadron under command of Captain Perry having met the British squadron of superior force, a sanguinary conflict ended in the capture of the whole. The conduct of that officer, adroit as it was daring, and which was so well seconded by his comrades, justly entitles them to the admiration and gratitude of their country, and will fill an early page in its naval annals with a victory never surpassed in luster, however much it may have been in magnitude.

On Lake Ontario the caution of the British commander, favored by contingencies, frustrated the efforts of the American commander to bring on a decisive action. Captain Chauncey was able, however, to establish an ascendency on that important theater, and to prove by the manner in which he effected everything possible that opportunities only were wanted for a more shining display of his own talents and the gallantry of those under his command.

The success on Lake Erie have opened a passage to the territory of the enemy, the officer commanding the Northwestern army transfered the war thither, and rapidly pursuing the hostile troops, fleeing with their savage associates, forced a general action, which quickly terminated in the capture of the British and dispersion of the savage force.

This result is signally honorable to Major-General Harrison, by whose military talents it was prepared; to Colonel Johnson and his mounted volunteers, whose impetuous onset gave a decisive blow to the ranks of the enemy, and to the spirit of the volunteer militia, equally brave and patriotic, who bore an interesting part in the scene; more especially to the chief magistrate of Kentucky, at the head of them, whose heroism signalized in the war which established the independence of his country, sought at an advanced age a share in hardships and battles for maintaining its rights and its safety.

The effect of these successes has been to rescue the inhabitants of Michigan from their oppressions, aggravated by gross infractions of the capitulation which subjected them to a foreign power; to alienate the savages of numerous tribes from the enemy, by whom they were disappointed and abandoned, and to relieve an extensive region of country from a merciless warfare which desolated its frontiers and imposed on its citizens the most harassing services.

In consequence of our naval superiority on Lake Ontario and the opportunity afforded by it for concentrating our forces by water, operations which had been provisionally planned were set on foot against the possessions of the enemy on the St. Lawrence. Such, however, was the delay produced in the first instance by adverse weather of unusual violence and continuance and such the circumstances attending the final movements of the army, that the prospect, at one time so favorable, was not realized.

The cruelty of the enemy in enlisting the savages into a war with a nation desirous of mutual emulation in mitigating its calamities has not been confined to any one quarter. Wherever they could be turned against us no exertions to effect it have been spared. On our southwestern border the Creek tribes, who, yielding to our persevering endeavors, were gradually acquiring more civilized habits, became the unfortunate victims of seduction. A war in that quarter has been the consequence, infuriated by a bloody fanaticism recently propagated among them. It was necessary to crush such a war before it could spread among the contiguous tribes and before it could favor enterprises of the enemy into that vicinity. With this view a force was called into the service of the United States from the States of Georgia and Tenessee, which, with the nearest regular troops and other corps from the Mississippi Territory, might not only chastise the savages into present peace but make a lasting impression on their fears.

The progress of the expedition, as far as is yet known, corresponds with the martial zeal with which it was espoused, and the best hopes of a satisfactory issue are authorized by the complete success with which a well-planned enterprise was executed against a body of hostile savages by a detachment of the volunteer militia of Tennessee, under the gallant command of General Coffee, and by a still more important victory over a larger body of them, gained under the immediate command of Major-General Jackson, an officer equally distinguished for his patriotism and his military talents.

The systematic perseverance of the enemy in courting the aid of the savages in all quarters had the natural effect of kindling their ordinary propensity to war into a passion, which, even among those best disposed toward the United States, was ready, if not employed on our side, to be turned against us. A departure from our protracted forbearance to accept the services tendered by them has thus been forced upon us. But in yielding to it the retaliation has been mitigated as much as possible, both in its extent and in its character, stopping far short of the example of the enemy, who owe the advantages they have occasionally gained in battle chiefly to the number of their savage associates, and who have not controlled them either from their usual practice of indiscriminate massacre on defenseless inhabitants or from scenes of carnage without a parallel on prisoners to the British arms, guarded by all the laws of humanity and of honorable war. For these enormities the enemy' are equally responsible, whether with the power to prevent them they want the will or with the knowledge of a want of power they still avail themselves of such instruments.

In other respects the enemy are pursuing a course which threatens consequences most afflicting to humanity.

A standing law of Great Britain naturalizes, as is well known, all aliens complying with conditions limited to a shorter period than those required by the United States, and naturalized subjects are in war employed by her Government in common with native subjects. In a contiguous British Province regulations promulgated since the commencement of the war compel citizens of the United States being there under certain circumstances to bear arms, whilst of the native emigrants from the United States, who compose much of the population of the Province, a number have actually borne arms against the United States within their limits, some of whom, after having done so, have become prisoners of war, and are now in our possession. The British commander in that Province, nevertheless, with the sanction, as appears, of his Government, thought proper to select from American prisoners of war and send to Great Britain for trial as criminals a number of individuals who had emigrated from the British dominions long prior to the state of war between the two nations, who had incorporated themselves into our political society in the modes recognized by the law and the practice of Great Britain, and who were made prisoners of war under the banners of their adopted country, fighting for its rights and its safety.

The protection due to these citizens requiring an effectual interposition in their behalf, a like number of British prisoners of war were put into confinement, with a notification that they would experience whatever violence might be committed on the American prisoners of war sent to Great Britain.

It was hoped that this necessary consequence of the step unadvisedly taken on the part of Great Britain would have led her Government to reflect on the inconsistencies of its conduct, and that a sympathy with the British, if not with the American, sufferers would have arrested the cruel career opened by its example.

This was unhappily not the case. In violation both of consistency and of humanity, American officers and noncommissioned officers in double the number of the British soldiers confined here were ordered into close confinement, with formal notice that in the event of a retaliation for the death which might be inflicted on the prisoners of war sent to Great Britain for trial the officers so confined would be put to death also. It was notified at the same time that the commanders of the British fleets and armies on our coasts are instructed in the same event to proceed with a destructive severity against our towns and their inhabitants.

That no doubt might be left with the enemy of our adherence to the retaliatory resort imposed on us, a correspondent number of British officers, prisoners of war in our hands, were immediately put into close confinement to abide the fate of those confined by the enemy, and the British Government has been apprised of the determination of this Government to retaliate any other proceedings against us contrary to the legitimate modes of warfare.

It is as fortunate for the United States that they have it in their power to meet the enemy in this deplorable contest as it is honorable to them that they do not join in it but under the most imperious obligations, and with the humane purpose of effectuating a return to the established usages of war.

The views of the French Government on the subjects which have been so long committed to negotiation have received no elucidation since the close of your late session. The minister plenipotentiary of the United States at Paris had not been enabled by proper opportunities to press the objects of his mission as prescribed by his instructions.

The militia being always to be regarded as the great bulwark of defense and security for free states, and the Constitution having wisely committed to the national authority a use of that force as the best provision against an unsafe military establishment, as well as a resource peculiarly adapted to a country having the extent and the exposure of the United States, I recommend to Congress a revision of the militia laws for the purpose of securing more effectually the services of all detachments called into the employment and placed under the Government of the United States.

It will deserve the consideration of Congress also whether among other improvements in the militia laws justice does not require a regulation, under due precautions, for defraying the expense incident to the first assembling as well as the subsequent movements of detachments called into the national service.

To give to our vessels of war, public and private, the requisite advantage in their cruises, it is of much importance that they should have, both for themselves and their prizes, the use of the ports and markets of friendly powers. With this view, I recommend to Congress the expediency of such legal provisions as may supply the defects or remove the doubts of the Executive authority, to allow to the cruisers of other powers at war with enemies of the United States such use of the American ports as may correspond with the privileges allowed by such powers to American cruisers.

During the year ending on the 30th of September last the receipts into the Treasury have exceeded $37,500,000 of which near twenty-four millions were the produce of loans. After meeting all demands for the public service there remained in the Treasury on that day near $7,000, 000. Under the authority contained in the act of the 2d of August last for borrowing $7,500,000, that sum has been obtained on terms more favorable to the United States than those of the preceding loan made during the present year. Further sums to a considerable amount will be necessary to be obtained in the same way during the ensuing year, and from the increased capital of the country, from the fidelity with which the public engagements have been kept and the public credit maintained, it may be expected on good grounds that the necessary pecuniary supplies will not be wanting.

The expenses of the current year, from the multiplied operations falling within it, have necessarily been extensive; but on a just estimate of the campaign in which the mass of them has been incurred the cost will not be found disproportionate to the advantages which have been gained. The campaign has, indeed, in its latter stages in one quarter been less favorable than was expected, but in addition to the importance of our naval success the progress of the campaign has been filled with incidents highly honorable to the American arms.

The attacks of the enemy on Craney Island, on Fort Meigs, on Sacketts Harobr, and on Sandusky have been vigorously and successfully repulsed; nor have they in any case succeeded on either frontier excepting when directed against the peaceable dwellings of individuals or villages unprepared or undefended.

On the other hand, the movements of the American Army have been followed by the reduction of York, and of Forts George, Erie, and Malden; by the recovery of Detroit and the extinction of the Indian war in the West, and by the occupancy or command of a large portion of Upper Canada. Battles have also been fought on the borders of the St. Lawrence, which, though not accomplishing their entire objects, reflect honor on the discipline and prowess of our soldiery, the best auguries of eventual victory. In the same scale are to be placed the late successes in the South over one of the most powerful, which had become one of the most hostile also, of the Indian tribes.

It would be improper to close this communication without expressing a thankfulness in which all ought to unite for the numerous blessings with which our beloved country continues to be favored; for the abundance which overspreads our land, and the prevailing health of its inhabitants; for the preservation of our internal tranquillity, and the stability of our free institutions, and, above all, for the light of divine truth and the protection of every man's conscience in the enjoyment of it. And although among our blessings we can not number an exemption from the evils of war, yet these will never be regarded as the greatest of evils by the friends of liberty and of the rights of nations. Our country has before preferred them to the degraded condition which was the alternative when the sword was drawn in the cause which give birth to our national independence, and none who contemplate the magnitude and feel the value of that glorious event will shrink from a struggle to maintain the high and happy ground on which it placed the American people.

With all good citizens the justice and necessity of resisting wrongs and usurpations no longer to be borne will sufficiently outweigh the privations and sacrifices inseparable from a state of war. But it is a reflection, moreover, peculiarly consoling, that, whilst wars are generally aggravated by their baneful effects on the internal improvements and permanent prosperity of the nations engaged in them, such is the favored situation of the United States that the calamities of the contest into which they have been compelled to enter are mitigated by improvements and advantages of which the contest itself is the source.

If the war has increased the interruptions of our commerce, it has at the same time cherished and multiplied our manufactures so as to make us independent of all other countries for the more essential branches for which we ought to be dependent on none, and is even rapidly giving them an extent which will create additional staples in our future intercourse with foreign markets.

If much treasure has been expended, no inconsiderable portion of it has been applied to objects durable in their value and necessary to our permanent safety.

If the war has exposed us to increased spoliations on the ocean and to predatory incursions on the land, it has developed the national means of retaliating the former and of providing protection against the latter, demonstrating to all that every blow aimed at our maritime independence is an impulse accelerating the growth of our maritime power.

By diffusing through the mass of the nation the elements of military discipline and instruction; by augmenting and distributing warlike preparations applicable to future use; by evincing the zeal and valor with which they will be employed and the cheerfulness with which every necessary burden will be borne, a greater respect for our rights and a longer duration of our future peace are promised than could be expected without these proofs of the national character and resources.

The war has proved moreover that our free Government, like other free governments, though slow in its early movements, acquires in its progress a force proportioned to its freedom, and that the union of these States, the guardian of the freedom and safety of all and of each, is strengthened by every occasion that puts it to the test.

In fine, the war, with all its vicissitudes, is illustrating the capacity and the destiny of the United States to be a great, a flourishing, and a powerful nation, worthy of the friendship which it is disposed to cultivate with all others, and authorized by its own example to require from all an observances of the laws of justice and reciprocity.

Beyond these their claims have never extended; and in contending for these we behold a subject for our congratulations in the daily testimonies of increasing harmony throughout the nation, and may humbly repose our trust in the smiles of Heaven on so righteous a cause.

JAMES MADISON

REQUEST FOR AN EMBARGO BILL
December 9, 1813

> *The embargo requested by Madison was directed ag-*
> *ainst Great Britain and its aim was to shorten the war*
> *by bringing pressure against the enemy. Congress*
> *acted with such suprising speed in giving the Presi-*
> *dent what he asked for that within eight days after*
> *asking for its passage he was able to sign the com-*
> *pleted bill.*

To the Senate and House of Representatives of the United States:
The tendency of our commercial and navigation laws in their present state to favor the enemy and thereby prolong the war is more
and more developed by experience. Supplies of the most essential
kinds find their way not only to British ports and British armies at
a distance, but the armies in our neighborhood with which our own
are contending derive from our ports and outlets a subsistence attainable with difficulty, if at all, from other sources. Even the fleets
and troops infesting our coasts and waters are by like supplies ac-
commodated and encouraged in their predatory and incursive warfare.

Abuses having a like tendency take place in our import trade. British fabrics and products find their way into our ports under the name
and from the ports of other countries, and often in British vessels
disguised as neutrals by false colors and papers.

To these abuses it may be added that illegal importations are openly
made with advantage to the violators of the law, produced by under-
valuations or other circumstances involved in the course of the judicial proceedings against them.

To these abuses it may be added that illegal importations are openly
made with advantage to the violators of the law, produced by under-
valuations or other circumstances involved in the course of the judicial proceedings against them.

It is found also that the practice of ransoming is a cover for collusive captures and a channel for intelligence advantageous to the
enemy.

To remedy as much as possible these evils, I recommend:

That an effectual embargo on exports be immediately enacted.

That all articles known to be derived, either not at all or in any
immaterial degree only, from the productions of any other country
than Great Britain, and particularly the extensive articles made of
wool and cotton materials, and ardent spirits made from the cane,
be expressly and absolutely prohibited, from whatever port of place
or in whatever vessels the same may be brought into the United

States, and that all violations of the nonimportation act be subjected to adequate penalties.

That among the proofs of the neutral and national character of foreign vessels it be required that the masters and supercargoes and three-fourths at least of the crews be citizens or subjects of the country under whose flag the vessle sail.

That all persons concerned in collusive captures by the enemy or in ransoming vessels or their cargoes from the enemy be subjected to adequate penalties.

To shorten as much as possible the duration of the war it is indispensable that the enemy should feel all the pressure that can be given to it, and the restraints having that tendency will be borne with the greater cheerfulness by all good citizens, as the restraints will affect those most who are most ready to sacrifice the interest of their country in pursuit of their own.

JAMES MADISON.

SIXTH ANNUAL MESSAGE
September 20, 1814

In this message, Madison listed the naval and land victories American forces had achieved over the British. He warned Congress, however, that the negotiations at Ghent were still in doubt and that the British gave every indication of continuing their hostility to the United States. It was necessary, therefore, for Congress to provide war funds and take measures to fill the regular army, classify the militia and enlarge the provision for special corps.

Fellow-Citizens of the Senate and of the House of Representatives:

Notwithstanding the early day which had been fixed for your session of the present year, I was induced to call you together still sooner, as well that any inadequacy in the existing provisions for the wants of the Treasury might be supplied as that no delay might happen in providing for the result of the negotiations on foot with Great Britain, whether it should require arrangements adapted to a return of peace or further and more effective provisions for prosecuting the war.

That result is not yet known. If, on the one hand, the repeal of the orders in council and the general pacification in Europe, which withdrew the occasion on which impressments from American vessels were practiced, suggest expectations that peace and amity may be reestablished, we are compelled, on the other hand, by the refusal of the British Government to accept the offered mediation of the Emperor of Russia, by the delays in giving effect to its own proposal of a direct negotiation, and, above all, by the principles and manner in which the war is now avowedly carried on to infer that a spirit of hostility is indulged more violent than ever against the rights and prosperity of this country.

This increased violence is best explained by the two important circumstances that the great contest in Europe for an equilibrium guaranteeing all its States against the ambition of any has been closed without any check on the overbearing power of Great Britain on the ocean, and it has left in her hands disposable armaments, with which, forgetting the difficulties of a remote war with a free people, and yielding to the intoxication of success, with the example of a great victim to it before her eyes, she cherishes hopes of still further aggrandizing a power already formidable in its abuses to the tranquillity of the civilized and commercial world.

But whatever may have inspired the enemy with these more violent purposes, the public councils of a nation more able to maintain than it was to acquire its independence, and with a devotion to it rendered more ardent by the experiences of its blessings, can never deliberate but on the means most effectual for defeating the extravagant views or unwarrantable passions with which alone the war can now be pursued against us.

In the events of the present campaign the enemy, with all his augmented means and wanton use of them, has little ground for exultation, unless he can feel it in the success of his recent enterprises against this metropolis and the neighboring town of Alexandria, from both of which his retreats were as precipitate as his attempts were bold and fortunate. In his other incursions on our Atlantic frontier his progress, often checked and chastised by the martial spirit of the neighboring citizens, has had more effect in distressing individuals and in dishonoring his arms than in promoting any object of legitimate warfare; and in the two instances mentioned, however deeply to be regretted on our part, he will find in his transient success, which interrupted for a moment only the ordinary public business at the seat of Government, no compensation for the loss of character with the world by his violations of private property and by his destruction of public edifices protected as monuments of the arts by the laws of civilized warfare.

On our side we can appeal to a series of achievements which have given new luster to the American arms. Besides the brilliant incidents in the minor operations of the campaign, the splendid victories gained on the Canadian side of the Niagara by the American forces under Major-General Brown and Brigadiers Scott and Gaines have gained for these heroes and their emulating companions the most unfading laurels, and, having triumphantly tested the progressive discipline of the American soldiery, have taught the enemy that the longer he protracts his hostile efforts the more certain and decisive will be his final discomfiture.

On our southern border victory has continued also to follow the American standard. The bold and skillful operations of Major-General Jackson, conducting troops drawn from the militia of the States least distant, particularly of Tennessee, have subdued the principal tribes of hostile savages, and, by establishing a peace with them, preceded by recent and exemplary chastisement, has best guarded against the mischief of their cooperation with the British enterprises which may be planned against that quarter of our country. Important tribes of Indians on our northwestern frontier have also acceded to stipulations which bind them to the interests of the United States and to consider our enemy as theirs also.

In the recent attempt of the enemy on the city of Baltimore, defended by militia and volunteers, aided by a small body of regulars and seamen, he was received with a spirit which produced a rapid retreat to his ships, whilst a concurrent attack by a large fleet was successfully resisted by the steady and well-directed fire of the fort and batteries opposed to it.

In another recent attack by a powerful force on our troops at Plattsburg, of which regulars made a part only, the enemy, after a perseverance for many hours, was finally compelled to seek safety in a hasty retreat, with our gallant bands pressing upon him.

On the Lakes, so much contested throughout the war, the great exertions for the command made on our part have been well repaid. On Lake Ontario our squadron is now and has been for some time in a condition to confine that of the enemy to his own port, and to favor the operations of our land forces on that frontier.

A part of the squadron on Lake Erie has been extended into Lake Huron, and has produced the advantage of displaying our command on that lake also. One object of the expedition was the reduction of Mackinaw, which failed with the loss of a few brave men, among whom was an officer justly distinguished for his gallant exploits. The expedition, ably conducted by both the land and the naval commanders, was otherwise highly valuable in its effects.

On Lake Champlain, where our superiority had for some time been undisputed, the British squadron lately came into action with the American, commanded by Captain Macdonough. It issued in the capture of the whole of the enemy's ships. The best praise for this officer and his intrepid comrades is in the likeness of his triumph to the illustrious victory which immortalized another officer and established at a critical moment our command of another lake.

On the ocean the pride of our naval arms had been amply supported. A second frigate has indeed fallen into the hands of the enemy, but the loss is hidden in the blaze of heroism with which she was defended. Captain Porter, who commanded her , and whose previous career had been distinguished by daring enterprise and by fertility of genius, maintained a sanguinary contest against two ships, one of them superior to his own, and under other severe disadvantages, till humanity tore down the colors which valor had nailed to the mast. This officer and his brave comrades have added much to the rising glory of the American flag, and have merited all the effusions of gratitude which their country is ever ready to bestow on the champions of its rights and of its safety.

Two smaller vessels of war have also become prizes to the enemy, but by a superiority of force which sufficiently vindicates the reputation of their commanders, whilst two others, one commanded by Captain Warrington, the other by Captain Blakely, have captured British ships of the same class with a gallantry and good conduct which entitle them and their companions to a just share in the praise of their country.

In spite of the naval force of the enemy accumulated on our coasts, our private cruisers also have not ceased to annoy his commerce and to bring their rich prizes into our ports, contributing thus, with other proofs to demonstrate the incompetency and illegality of a blockade the proclamation of which is made the pretext for vexing and discouraging the commerce of neutral powers with the United States.

To meet the extended and diversified warfare adopted by the enemy, great bodies of militia have been taken into service for the public defense, and great expenses incurred. That the defense everywhere may be both more convenient and more economical, Congress will see the necessity of immediate measures for filling the ranks of the Regular Army and of enlarging the provision for special corps, mounted and unmounted, to be engaged for longer periods of service than are due from the militia. I earnestly renew, at the same time, a recommendation of such changes in the system of the militia as, by classing and disciplining for the most prompt and active service the portions most capable of it, will give to that great resource for the public safety all the requisite energy and efficiency.

The moneys received into the Treasury during the nine months ending on the 30th day of June last amounted to $32,000,000, of which near eleven millions were the proceeds of the public revenue and the remainder derived from loans. The disbursements for public expenditures during the same period exceeded $34,000,000, and left in the Treasury on the 1st day of July near $5,000,000. The demands during the remainder of the present year already authorized by Congress and the expenses incident to an extension of the operations of the war will render it necessary that large sums should be provided to meet them.

From this view of the national affairs Congress will be urged to take up without delay as well the subject of pecuniary supplies as that of military force, and on a scale commensurate with the extent and the character which the war has assumed. It is not to be disguised that the situation of our country calls for its greatest efforts. Our enemy is powerful in men and in money, on the land and on the water. Availing himself of fortuitous advantages, he is aiming with his undivided force a deadly blow at our growing prosperity, perhaps at our national existence. He has avowed his purpose of trampling on the usages of civilized warfare, and given earnests of it in the plunder and wanton destruction of private property. In his pride of maritime dominion and in his thirst of commercial monopoly he strikes with peculiar animosity at the progress of our navigation and of our manufactures. His barbarous policy has not even spared those monuments of the arts and models of taste with which our country had enriched and embellished its infant metropolis. From such an adversary hostility in its greatest force and in its worst forms may be looked for. The American people will face it with the undaunted spirit which in their revolutionary struggle defeated his unrighteous projects. His threats and his barbarities, instead of dismay, will kindle in every bosom an indignation not to be extinguished but in the disaster and expulsion of such cruel invaders. In providing the means necessary the National Legislature will not distrust the heroic and enlightened patriotism of its constituents. They will cheerfully and proudly bear every burden of every kind which the safety and honor of the nation demand. We have seen them everywhere paying their taxes, direct and indirect, with the greatest promptness and alacrity. We see them rushing with enthusiasm to the scenes where danger and duty call. In offering their blood they give the surest pledge that no other tribute will be withheld.

Having forborne to declare war until to other aggressions had been added the capture of nearly a thousand American vessels and the impressment of thousands of American seafaring citizens, and until a final declaration had been made by the Government of Great Britain that her hostile orders against our commerce would not be revoked but on conditions as impossible as unjust, whilst it was known that these orders would not otherwise cease but with a war which had lasted nearly twenty years, and which, according to appearances at that time, might last as many more; having manifested on every occasion and in every proper mode a sincere desire to arrest the effusion of blood and meet our enemy on the ground of justice and reconciliation, our beloved country, in still opposing to his persevering hostility all its energies, with an undiminished disposition toward peace and friendship on honorable terms, must carry with it the good wishes of the impartial world and the best hopes of support from an omnipotent and kind Providence.

JAMES MADISON.

SEVENTH ANNUAL MESSAGE
December 5, 1815

This message marked the first time since Madison be-
came President that he was able to address Congress
in terms of the country's welfare rather than under
pressure of some present or impending crisis. Noting
that the country now had a commercial treaty with
England and that relations with Indian tribes were
generally tranquil, Madison turned his attention to
such matters as the adjustment of import duties and
the building of roads and canals.

Fellow-Citizens of the Senate and of the House of Representatives:
I have the satisfaction on our present meeting of being able to
communicate to you the successful termination of the war which had
been commenced against the United States by the Regency of Algiers.
The squadron in advance on that service, under Commodore Decatur,
lost not a moment after its arrival in the Mediterranean in seeking
the naval force of the enemy then cruising in that sea, and succeeded
in capturing two of his ships, one of them the principal ship, commanded by the Algerine admiral. The high character of the American
commander was brilliantly sustained on the occasion which brought his
own ship into close action with that of his adversary, as was the ac-
customed gallantry of all the officers and men actually engaged. Having prepared the way by this demonstration of American skill and
prowess, he hastened to the port of Algiers, where peace was promptly
yielded to his victorious force. In the terms stipulated the rights and
honor of the United States were particularly consulted by a perpetual
relinquishment on the part of the Dey of all pretensions to tribute
from them. The impressions which have thus been made, strengthened
as they will have been by subsequent transactions with the Regencies
of Tunis and of Tripoli by the appearance of the larger force which
followed under Commodore Bainbridge, the chief in command of the
expedition, and by the judicious precautionary arrangements left by
him in that quarter, afford a reasonable prospect of future security
for the valuable portion of our commerce which passes within reach
of the Barbary cruisers.

It is another source of satisfaction that the treaty of peace with
Great Britain has been succeeded by a convention on the subject of
commerce concluded by the plenipotentiaries of the two countries.
In this result a disposition is manifested on the part of that nation
corresponding with the disposition of the United States, which it may
be hoped will be improved into liberal arrangements on other subjects
on which the parties have mutual interests, or which might endanger
their future harmony. Congress will decide on the expediency of pro-

moting such a sequel by giving effect to the measure of confining the American navigation to American seamen—a measure which, at the same time that it might have that conciliatory tendency, would have the further advantage of increasing the independence of our navigation and the resources for our maritime defense.

In conformity with the articles in the treaty of Ghent relating to the Indians, as well as with a view to the tranquillity of our western and northwestern frontiers, measures were taken to establish an immediate peace with the several tribes who had been engaged in hostilities against the United States. Such of them as were invited to Detroit acceded readily to a renewal of the former treaties of friendship. Of the other tribes who were invited to a station on the Mississippi the greater number have also accepted the peace offered to them. The residue, consisting of the more distant tribes or parts of tribes, remain to be brought over by further explanations, or by such other means as may be adapted to the dispositions they may finally disclose.

The Indian tribes within and bordering on the southern frontier, whom a cruel war on their part had compelled us to chastise into peace, have latterly shown a restlessness which has called for preparatory measures for repressing it, and for protecting the commissioners engaged in carrying the terms of the peace into execution.

The execution of the act for fixing the military peace establishment has been attended with difficulties which even now can only be overcome by legislative aid. The selection of officers, the payment and discharge of the troops enlisted for the war, the payment of the retained troops and their reunion from detached and distant stations, the collection and security of the public property in the Quartermaster, Commissary, and Ordnance departments, and the constant medical assistance required in hospitals and garrisons rendered a complete execution of the act impracticable on the 1st of May, the period more immediately contemplated. As soon, however, as circumstances would permit, and as far as it has been practicable consistently with the public interests, the reduction of the Army has been accomplished; but the appropriations for its pay and for other branches of the military service having proved inadequate, the earliest attention to that subject will be necessary; and the expediency of continuing upon the peace establishment the staff officers who have hitherto been provisionally retained is also recommended to the consideration of Congress.

In the performance of the Executive duty upon this occasion there has not been wanting a just sensibility to the merits of the American Army during the late war; but the obvious policy and design in fixing an efficient military peace establishment did not afford an opportunity to distinguish the aged and infirm on account of their past services nor the wounded and disabled on account of their present sufferings.

The extent of the reduction, indeed, unavoidably involved the exclusion of many meritorious officers of every rank from the service of their country; and so equal as well as so numerous were the claims to attention that a decision by the standard of comparative merit could seldom be attained. Judged, however, in candor by a general standard of positive merit, the Army Register will, it is believed, do honor to the establishment, while the case of those officers whose names are not included in its devolves with the strongest interest upon the legislative authority for such provision as shall be deemed the best calculated to give support and solace to the veteran and the invalid, to display the beneficence as well as the justice of the Government, and to inspire a martial zeal for the public service upon every future emergency.

Although the embarrassments arising from the want of an uniform national currency have not been diminished since the adjournment of Congress, great satisfaction has been derived in contemplating the revival of the public credit and the efficiency of the public resources. The receipts into the Treasury from the various branches of revenue during the nine months ending on the 30th of September last have been estimated at $12,500,000; the issues of Treasury notes of every denomination during the same period amounted to the sum of $14,-000,000, and there was also obtained upon loan during the same period a sum of $9,000,000, of which the sum of $6,000,000 was subscribed in cash and the sum of $3,000,000 in Treasury notes. With these means added to the sum of $1,500,000, being the balance of money in the Treasury on the 1st day of January, there has been paid between the 1st of January and the 1st of October on account of the appropriations of the preceding and of the present year (exclusively of the amount of the Treasury notes subscribed to the loan and of the amount redeemed in the payment of duties and taxes) the aggregate sum of $33,500,000, including the interest on the public debt payable on the 1st of January next, will be demanded at the Treasury to complete the expenditures of the present year, and for which the existing ways and means will sufficiently provide.

The national debt, as it was ascertained on the 1st of October last, amounted in the whole to the sum of $120,000,000, consisting of the unredeemed balance of the debt contracted before the late war ($39,-000,000), the amount of the funded debt contracted in consequence of the war ($64,000,000), and the amount of the unfunded and floating debt, including the various issues of Treasury notes, $17,000,000 which is in a gradual course of payment. There will probably be some addition to the public debt upon the liquidation of various claims which are depending, and a conciliatory disposition on the part of Congress may lead honorably and advantageously to an equitable arrangement of the militia expenses incurred by the several States without the previous sanction or authority of the Government of the United States; but when it is considered that the new as well as the old portion of the debt has been contracted in the assertion of the national rights and independence, and when it is recollected that the public expenditures, not being exclusively bestowed upon subjects of a transient nature, will long be visible in the number and equipments of the American Navy, in the military works for the defense of our harbors and our frontiers, and in the supplies of our arsenals and magazines the amount will bear a gratifying comparison with the objects which have been attained, as well as with the resources of the country.

The arrangements of the finances with a view to the receipts and expenditures of a permanent peace establishment will necessarily enter into the deliberations of Congress during the present session. It is true that the improved condition of the public revenue will not only afford the means of maintaining the faith of the Government with its creditors inviolate, and of prosecuting successfully the measures of the most liberal policy, but will also justify an immediate alleviation of the burdens imposed by the necessities of the war. It is, however, essential to every modification of the finances that the benefits of an uniform national currency should be restored to the community. The absence of the precious metals will, it is believed, be a temporary evil, but until they can again be rendered the general medium of exchange it devolves on the wisdom of Congress to provide a substitute which shall equally engage the confidence and accomodate the wants of the citizens throughout the Union. If the operation of the State banks can not produce this result, the probable operation of a national bank will merit consideration; and if neither of these expedients be deemed effectual it may become necessary to ascertain the terms upon which the notes of the Government (no longer required as an instrument of credit) shall be issued upon motives of general policy as a common medium of circulation.

Notwithstanding the security for future repose which the United States ought to find in their love of peace and their constant respect for the rights of other nations, the character of the times particularly inculcates the lesson that, whether to prevent or repel danger, we ought not to be unprepared for it. This consideration will sufficiently recommend to Congress a liberal provision for the immediate extension and gradual completion of the works of defense, both fixed and flaoting, on our maritime frontier, and an adequate provision for guarding our inland frontier against dangers to which certain portions of it may continue to be exposed.

As an improvement in our military establishment, it will deserve the consideration of Congress whether a corps of invalid might not be so organized and employed as at once to aid in the support of meritorious individuals excluded by age or infirmities from the existing establishment, and to procure to the public the benefit of their stationary services and of their exemplary discipline. I recommend also an enlargement of the Military Academy already established, and the establishment of others in other sections of the Union; and I can not press too much on the attention of Congress such a classification and organization of the militia as will most effectually render it the safeguard of a free state. If experience has shewn in the recent splendid achievements of militia the value of this resource for the public defense, it has shewn also the importance of that skill in the use of arms and that familiarity with the essential rules of discipline which can not be expected from the regulations now in force. With this subject is intimately connected the necessity of accommodating the laws in every respect to the great object of enabling the political authority of the Union to employ promptly and effectually the physical power of the Union in the cases designated by the Constitution.

The signal services which have been rendered by our Navy and the capacities it has developed for successful cooperation in the national defense will give to that portion of the public force its full value in the eyes of Congress, at an epoch which calls for the constant viligilance of all governments. To preserve the ships now in a sound state, to complete those already contemplated, to provide amply the imperishable materials for prompt augmentations, and to improve the existing arrangements into more advantageous establishments for the construction, the repairs, and the security of vessels of war is dictated by the soundest policy.

In adjusting the duties on imports to the object of revenue the influence of the tariff on manufactures will necessarily present itself for consideration. However wise the theory may be which leaves to the sagacity and interest of individuals the application of their industry and resources, there are in this as in other cases exceptions to the general rule. Besides the condition which the theory itself implies of a reciprocal adoption by other nations, experience teaches that so many circumstances must concur in introducing and maturing manufacturing establishments, especially of the more complicated kinds, that a country may remain long without them, although sufficiently advanced and in some respects even peculiarly fitted for carrying them on with success. Under circumstances giving a powerful impulse to manufacturing industry it has made among us a progress and exhibited an efficiency which justify the belief that with a protection not more than is due to the enterprising citizens whose interests are now at stake it will become at an early day not only safe against occasional competitions from abroad, but a source of domestic wealth and even of external commerce. In selecting the branches more especially entitled to the public patronage a preference is obviously claimed by such as will relieve the United States from a dependence on foreign supplies, ever subject to casual failures, for articles necessary for the public defense or connected with the primary wants of individuals. It will be an additional recommendation of particular manufactures where the materials for them are extensively drawn from our agriculture, and consequently impart and insure to that great fund of national prosperity and independence an encouragement which can not fail to be rewarded.

Among the means of advancing the public interest the occasion is a proper one for recalling the attention of Congress to the great importance of establishing throughout our country the roads and canals which can best be executed under the national authority. No objects within the circle of political economy so richly repay the expense bestowed on them; there are none the utility of which is more universally ascertained and acknowledged; none that do more honor to the governments whose wise and enlarged patriotism duly appreciates them. Nor is there any country which presents a field where nature invites more the art of man to complete her own work for his accommodation and benefit. These considerations are strengthened, moreover, by the political effect of these facilities for intercommunication in bringing and binding more closely together the various parts of our extended confederacy. Whilst the States individually, with a laudable enterprise and emulation, avail themselves of their local advantages by new roads, by navigable canals, and by improving the streams susceptible of navigation, the General Government is the more urged to similar undertakings, requiring a national jurisdiction and national means, by the prospect of thus systematically completing so inestimable a work; and it is a happy reflection that any defect of constitutional authority which may be encountered can be supplied in a mode which the Constitution itself has providently pointed out.

The present is a favorable season also for bringing again into view the establishment of a national seminary of learning within the District of Columbia, and with means drawn from the property therein, subject to the authority of the General Government. Such an institution claims the patronage of Congress as a monument of their solicitude for the advancement of knowledge, without which the blessings of liberty can not be fully enjoyed or long preserved; as a model instructive in the formation of other seminaries; as a nursery of enlightened preceptors, and as a central resort of youth and genius from every part of their country, diffusing on their return examples of those national feelings, those liberal sentiments, and those congenial manners which contribute cement to our Union and strength to the great political fabric of which that is the foundation.

In closing this communication I ought not to repress a sensibility, in which you will unite, to the happy lot of our country and to the goodness of a superintending Providence, to which we are indebted for it. Whilst other portions of mankind are laboring under the distresses of war or struggling with adversity in other forms, the United States are in the tranquil enjoyment of prosperous and honorable peace. In reviewing the scenes through which it has been attained we can rejoice in the proofs given that our political institutions, founded in human rights and framed for their preservation, are equal to the severest trials of war, as well as adapted to the ordinary periods of repose. As fruits of this experience and of the reputation acquired by the American arms on the land and on the water, the nation finds itself possessed of a growing respect abroad and of a just confidence in itself, which are among the best pledges for its peaceful career. Under other aspects of our country the strongest features of its flourishing condition are seen in a population rapidly increasing on a territory as productive as it is extensive; in a general industry and fertile ingenuity which find their ample rewards, and in an affluent revenue which admits a reduction of the public burdens without withdrawing the means of sustaining the public credit, of gradually discharging the public debt, of providing for the necessary defensie and precautionary establishments, and of patronizing in every authorized mode undertakings conducive to the aggregate wealth and individual comfort of our citizens.

It remains for the guardian of the public welfare to persevere in that justice and good will toward other nations which invite a return of these sentiments toward the United States; to cherish institutions which guarantee their safety and their liberties, civil and religious; and to combine with a liberal system of foreign commerce an improvement of the national advantages and a protection and extension of the independent resources of our highly favored and happy country.

In all measures having such objects my faithful cooperation will be afforded.

JAMES MADISON.

Bibliographical Aids

The emphasis in this and subsequent volumes in the Presidential Chronologies will be on the administrations of the Presidents. The more important works on other aspects of their lives, either before or after their terms, are included since they may contribute to an understanding of the Presidential careers.

The following bibliography is critically selected. Although there are many titles not included in this bibliography, an attempt has been made to list important books which can be found in most small to medium sized libraries. Large metropolitan libraries and those in colleges or universities, of course, will contain many titles not listed below. The student might also wish to consult *Reader's Guide to Periodical Literature and Social Sciences and Humanities Index* (formerly *International Index)* for recent articles in scholarly journals.

Additional chronological information not included in this volume because it did not relate directly to the President may be found in the *Encyclopaedia of American History,* edited by Richard B. Morris, revised edition (New York, 1965).

SOURCE MATERIALS

The student will find a wealth of published information about James Madison — not necessarily in biographies (for, unfortunately, there seem to be few full length works on Madison's life), but on important aspects of his public life.

It is almost impossible, for example, to find a book about the making of the Constitution that does not deal at length with Madison's political philosophy, since it is Madison who is acknowledged to be the "Father of the Constitution." The same can be said of any book on the Founding Fathers, the birth of the American Republic, the War of 1812, or individual biographies of Jefferson, Hamilton and John Adams. The truth of the matter is that throughout most of his adult life Madison played such an influential role in the affairs of the infant Republic that it is difficult to read *anything* about those early years without sooner or later encountering him or his ideas.

Madison himself left a large body of published material in the form of political articles and, of course, official documents. Often, however, Madison hid behind a cloak of anonymity. His many articles for *The*

Federalist, all written under the pseudonym "Publius," is a good example.

Happily enough, the student will find numerous recent titles which bear on the activities of James Madison. Very probably this is because the accomplishments and ideas of Madison—for example, the Constitution and the very essence of American democracy—continue to play a vital role in modern society. Madison still challenges present day scholars' and for this reason he has escaped the fate assigned to many past Presidents—that of being relegated to some distant corner of the library and being represented by a handful of outmoded books.

Madison, James. *The Federalist: A Commentary on the Constitution of the United States.* New York, 1941. Although there are many published versions of *The Federalist,* this publication by The Modern Library can be found in most libraries and bookstores. The author of each article (Madison, Hamilton or Jay) is identified.

Farrand, Max, ed. *The Records of the Federal Convention of 1787.* 3 vols., New Haven, 1937. Since Madison wrote the records for most of the convention, these volumes can be a valuable source for an examination of Madison's writing style. Let the student beware, though: These records are filled with the most minute detail which can be of little interest to anyone but the serious student. The records have been edited in chronological order.

BIOGRAPHIES

Brant, Irving. *The Life of James Madison.* 6 vols., New York, 1941-61. These six volumes more than make up for the fact that few authors have written biographies of M dison. Brant has written what is certainly the definitive work on the fourth President. No detail has been omitted, no clue left unfollowed concerning Madison's public or private life. Although the author's sympathy to Madison colors all six volumes, the student can be reasonably sure that what he reads here is correct. The student will also find that Brant is the possessor of a clear and lively writing style.

Gay, Sydney Howard. *James Madison.* Boston, 1885. A serviceable biography, although somewhat dated.

SPECIAL AREAS

Adams, Henry. *The Formative Years: A History of the United States during the Administrations of Jefferson and Madison,* Vol. 2, Boston, 1947. A detailed account of Madison's years in office, with heavy emphasis on the War of 1812. There are several published versions of Adams' work, including an abridged edition published in 1967 by the University of Chicago Press.

Bowen, Catherine Drinker. *Miracle at Philadelphia; The Story of the Constitutional Convention, May to September 1787*, Boston, 1966. Excellent account of the Convention, with many details pertaining to Madison's contributions.

Brown, Roger L. *The Republic in Peril: 1812*. New York, 1964. This book deals with the American decision to declare war on Great Britain. Primarily interested in the motives of the American executive and members of Congress who stood for or against the war, the author examines closely Madison's role in the events leading up to the declaration of war. This book is based on much new material found in libraries, archives and historical societies.

Donovan, Frank. *Mr. Madison's Constitution*. New York, 1965. A sympathetic account of Madison's role in the writing of the Constitution. It covers not only the work on the Convention itself, but also Madison's efforts to bring the Convention into being and his contribution as chief chronicler of the Convention.

Dos Passos, John. *The Men Who Made the Nation*. Garden City, 1957. The biographical details provided by the author include descriptions of appearance and personal habits not often found in historical works. All in all, a highly readable book.

------------------------*The Shackles of Power: Three Jeffersonian Decades*. Garden City, 1966. Although the author concentrates on Jefferson, he manages to weave in a wealth of material about Madison, Monroe and John Quincy Adams.

Engelman, Fred L. *The Peace of Christmas Eve*. New York, 1960. This book concentrates on the Treaty of Ghent and on the three men who undertook the negotiations—Gallatin, Bayard and John Quincy Adams. Madison's feelings about the treaty are discussed in some detail.

Johnson, Allen. *Union and Democracy*. Boston, 1915. A straightforward account of the first days of the Republic, from the writing of the Constitution to about 1825.

Koch, Adrienne. *Madison's "Advice to My Country."* Princeton, 1966. At the age of 83, Madison wrote a short document which he intended to be given posthumously to the nation. Using this 149-word document as a base, the author proceeds to a discussion of liberty, justice and union as Madison viewed them. Useful for an understanding of Madison's political philosophy.

Rossiter, Clinton. *1787, The Grand Convention.* New York, 1966. An acount of one year during which the Constitution was born. In the opinion of the author, 1787 was the "most fateful year in the history of the United States." This book, written by one of America's foremost historians, depicts the setting, men, events, finished work and struggle for ratification.

Tully, Andrew. *When They Burned the White House.* New York, 1965. A lively account of the British attack on Washington, with many details of Madison's actions.

ESSAYS

Bemis, Samuel F. *The American Secretaries of State and Their Diplomacy.* Vol 3, New York, 1927. A detailed study of Madison's actions while serving in Jefferson's cabinet.

Fiske, John. *Essays Historical and Literary.* Vol. 1, New York, 1907. A good capsule biography of Madison, his life, philosophy and accomplishments.

Koch, Adrienne. "James Madison and the Politics of Republicanism," in *The Federalists vs. the Jefferson Republicans.* Edited by Paul Goodman, New York, 1967. Deals with Madison's political philosophy, particularly in relation to Hamilton.

Perkins, Bradford. "Madison Was a Failure," in *The Causes of the War of 1812; National Honor or National Interest?* Edited by Bradford Perkins, New York, 1962. In this essay, Madison is pictured as a weak man with no control of either Congress or his cabinet, who allowed the United States to drift into war.

THE PRESIDENCY

Bailey, Thomas A. *Presidential Greatness: The Image and the Man from George Washington to the Present.* New York, 1966. A critical and subjective study of the qualities of Presidential greatness, arranged topically rather than chronologically.

Binkley, Wilfred E. *The Man in the White House: His Powers and Duties.* Revised ed., New York, 1964. Treats the development of the various roles of the American President.

Brown, Stuart Gerry. *The American Presidency: Leadership, Partisanship and Popularity.* New York, 1966. Seems to like the more partisan Presidents like Jefferson and Jackson.

Corwin, Edward S. *The President: Office and Powers*. 4th ed., New York, 1957. An older classic.

Kane, Joseph Nathan. *Facts About the Presidents*. New York, 1959. Included comparative as well as biographical data about the Presidents.

Koenig, Louis W. *The Chief Executive*. New York, 1964. Authoritative study of Presidential powers.

Laski, Harold J. *The American Presidency*. New York, 1940. A classic.

Rossiter, Clinton. *The American Presidency*. 2nd ed., New York, 1960. Useful.

Schlesinger, Arthur Meier. "Historians Rate United States Presidents," *Life*, XXV, November 1, 1948, 65ff.

--------------------------"Our Presidents: A Rating by Seventy-five Historians," *New York Times Magazine*, July 29, 1962, 12ff.

NAME INDEX

TITLES IN THE OCEANA
PRESIDENTIAL CHRONOLOGY SERIES

Reference books containing Chronology — Documents — Bibliographical Aids for each President covered.

Series Editor: Howard F. Bremer

*   96 pages, $3.00/B, available now.
** 128 pages, $4.00/B, available now.
*** 160 pages, $5.00/B, available late 1969.